First published in Great Britain in 2025 by

Greenfinch
An imprint of Quercus Editions Ltd
Carmelite House
50 Victoria Embankment
London EC4Y 0DZ

An Hachette UK company

Text copyright © 2025 Georgia White

The moral right of to Georgia White to be identified as the author of this work has been asserted in accordance with the Copyright, Designs and Patents Act, 1988.

All rights reserved. No part of this publication may be reproduced or transmitted in any form or by any means, electronic or mechanical, including photocopy, recording, or any information storage and retrieval system, without permission in writing from the publisher.

A CIP catalogue record for this book is available from the British Library

HB ISBN 978-1-52943-501-6
Ebook ISBN 978-1-52943-502-3

Quercus Editions Ltd hereby exclude all liability to the extent permitted by law for any errors or omissions in this book and for any loss, damage or expense (whether direct or indirect) suffered by a third party relying on any information contained in this book.

10 9 8 7 6 5 4 3 2 1

Design by Francesca Corsini
Illustrations by Trisha Srivastava

Printed and bound in China

Papers used by Greenfinch are from well-managed forests and other responsible sources.

THE LIFE-CHANGING POWER OF
TAROT

Reading the cards for self-empowerment

GEORGIA WHITE

greenfinch

Introduction	6
The Basics of Tarot	10
Choosing the Right Deck For You	18
Setting Up Your Environment	20
Numerology in Tarot Readings	22
Putting the Basics Together	24
Interaction Between Cards	27
Beginner Tarot Spreads	30
Tips for Reading Spreads	36
THE MAJOR ARCANA	**38**
The Fool	40
The Magician	44
The High Priestess	48
The Empress	52
The Emperor	56
The Hierophant	60
The Lovers	64
The Chariot	68
Strength	72
The Hermit	76
The Wheel of Fortune	79

Justice	83
The Hanged Man	87
Death	91
Temperance	93
The Devil	97
The Tower	101
The Star	104
The Moon	108
The Sun	112
Judgment	116
The World	119
THE MINOR ARCANA	122
Wands	124
Swords	152
Cups	186
Coins	216
A Self-Care Spread Example	248
Index	254
Acknowledgements	256

CONTENTS

INTRODUCTION

So, if you are here, it means you are on a very exciting journey of self-discovery, and what better way to continue this than by learning the beautiful art of reading tarot?

Believe it or not, you do not need to be 'psychic' to gain all the incredible insight that tarot cards have to offer. You may hear the word 'tarot' and immediately think of a fortune teller with a crystal ball . . . but there is so much more to tarot than meets the eye. Even though there is always a chance that you might 'cross paths with an interesting person' or 'suddenly come into a great deal of money', tarot can also offer an in-depth look at the behaviours and thought patterns you are engaging in and how they are impacting your experience of the world around you. It does not matter whether you currently believe in a higher power or not. You can use this guide as a valuable tool to check in with yourself and find out what is influencing you and how you can take back control of your own emotional state and sense of direction.

Whether you are a witch, a CEO, a student or a stay-at-home mum, tarot does not discriminate and has an abundance of knowledge for all. Instead of feeling like a victim of circumstance, you can use this guide to find empowerment from your experiences and forge a better path for yourself moving forwards.

There is a reason millions of people have turned to tarot for insight and guidance over the last few centuries . . . had it not been insightful or valuable, it would have disappeared a long time ago.

MY JOURNEY

I first discovered tarot when was just 14 years old and I have been on a whirlwind ride ever since. The cards have helped me navigate through so many difficult periods in my own life – big career changes, relocations abroad, overcoming mental health struggles and finding my way through the loss of loved ones – and they can help you too.

When my mum passed away, I learned how to embrace grief and honour the emotions I was experiencing. I was able to find closure and make important connections that would not have been able to make without insight from the cards.

When faced with big career or life decisions, tarot helped me to understand which instincts I have been acting on and whether they are impulsive or intuitive. It has helped me to understand how each decision I make can impact my future, and has encouraged me to take risks at the most opportune times or to hold back when something needed further investigation.

When facing hurdles with my mental health, tarot has showed me the tools I needed and helped me find direction, highlighting my strengths and weaknesses. It showed me the things I needed to prioritize moving forwards and gave me an action plan that allowed me to feel in control.

Tarot gave me the empowerment I needed to break through so many repetitive cycles in my own life and inspired me to build a network of more than a million people to share this self-empowerment journey with.

I first started posting collective tarot readings on TikTok in 2020 when I was experiencing great adversity in my life. At the beginning of the year, I had taken the plunge to move to Australia and was the happiest I had ever been. I was a newly qualified personal trainer, excited to help people feel confident in their own skin, and I could not wait to get started. A few weeks later I broke my arm, leaving me with no prospect of work. Three days after that, I learned that my childhood best friend had suddenly passed away. I flew back to the UK for three days so that I could attend her memorial service and then the whole world went into lockdown, and I could not return to my new home, or any of my belongings.

I lost many things at the beginning of 2020 but the one thing I did not lose was my passion for self-empowerment and I honestly do not know how I would have got through those months if I had not gained all of the insight that my tarot cards offered me.

Instead of asking about my future, I started asking such questions as: What can I learn from this experience? What will be the most helpful thing for me right now? What do I need to keep in mind moving forward? And this is when my perspective began to shift. I have even designed a specialized self-empowerment tarot spread for you to use in your own practice (see page 32).

Going from penniless, broken and grieving to receiving multiple job offers, exploring exciting new connections and getting my very own apartment, I knew I needed to share this approach with the world. I started to host live streams and post collective readings on TikTok and grew a following of more than 1.3 million people who gained a lot from the advice that came through from the cards.

And now you can too!

THE BASICS OF TAROT

A tarot deck is made up of 78 cards that each have their own unique meaning. The deck needs to be shuffled (normally with a question or intention in mind) and a selection of cards chosen at random during the shuffling process – sometimes simply falling out of the deck as you shuffle. Reading into the imagery, placement and knowledge of the cards reveals the bigger picture of what is going on and suggests helpful approaches for moving forwards.

Each card's suit represents an area of your life to reflect on. The number of the card asks you to consider how far into the process you are and the imagery hints at the bigger picture. You can find out what is influencing, hindering, motivating or challenging you. And you can look at relationships, career choices, bereavements, financial investments and so much more.

A tarot deck is split into two main categories: the Major Arcana and the Minor Arcana.

THE MAJOR ARCANA

The first 22 cards that make up any traditional tarot deck belong to the Major Arcana. These are standalone cards that each have their own individual names/meanings and represent the more major life events, lessons, behaviours or breakthroughs that we experience. At times, they can also represent important aspects of people we meet on our journey through life.

Pay extra attention to any Major Arcana cards that come through in a reading as these tend to represent the important themes and will give you a clear idea of what will be most helpful moving forwards. If several Major Arcana cards appear in a reading, this suggests that you are going through a particularly significant or intense chapter of your life. Massive changes or breakthroughs may be taking place or will need to take place in order for you to progress forwards.

THE MINOR ARCANA

The Minor Arcana consists of the remaining 56 cards in the tarot deck and are just like a normal pack of playing cards. There are four suits: Wands, Swords, Cups and Coins.
Each suit has its own unique energy, explained in detail below. Memorizing this can help you to read the cards later.

WANDS

What do you think of when you hear the word 'wand'? Magic, right? If you could wave a wand and ask for anything you want, what would it be? These cards represent your goals, desires, ambitions and purpose. Because Wands represent what sparks, fuels and inspires you, these cards are often associated with Fire signs such as Aries, Leo and Sagittarius. The cards do not indicate a specific star sign is relevant, but are more a representation of their qualities. Fire signs are passionate, courageous, go-getters. They are driven by instinct and represent the things we naturally feel drawn to or passionate about. When out of balance these individuals can seem aggressive, competitive, hesitant, insecure or impulsive. Wand cards might represent the opportunities or blockages you find yourself facing in this area.

> ✕ **KEY WORDS** ✕
> Fire signs · Action · Passion · Goals · Drive
> Desire · Ambition · Attraction

SWORDS

What do you think of when you hear the word 'sword'? Cut! Swords cut through the bull****. These cards represent clarity, finding solutions, information, thought processes, ideas and learning the truth.

Because this suit represents logic and mental processing, it is often associated with the Air signs, Gemini, Libra and Aquarius. They are direct and get straight to the point (a bit like a sword!).

These signs are intellectual in nature, have strong communication skills and are great with analytical creativity. When out of balance, these cards suggest untruthfulness, a lack of clarity, confusion, polarizing interests or conflict. These cards can signify some of the opportunities or blockages that you might face in this area. They may also represent some of the people that will share this journey or experience with you, who will either help or hinder you.

× KEY WORDS ×
Air signs · Logic · Reason · Thoughts · Beliefs · Ideas
Wit · Sharpness · Clarity

CUPS

What do you think of when you hear the word 'cup'? Water! Cups are vessels and, as such, they are associated with water, which is known to represent our emotions. These cards stand for the things in our lives that we are emotionally invested in. Because Cups are associated with water they also have links with Water signs such as Pisces, Cancer and Scorpio. Water signs are intuitive, sensitive and in touch with their emotional side. They are adaptable, flexible and mysterious. When out of balance, these signs can be emotionally overwhelmed, isolated, immature, manipulative, untrusting or sometimes even deceptive. These cards can represent some of the opportunities or blockages that you might face in this area, and might also hint at some of the people that will share this journey or experience with you such as family members, friendships or romantic partners.

> ✕ **KEY WORDS** ✕
> Water signs · Emotions · Flexibility · Adaptability · Fulfilment
> Connection · Family and Friends

COINS

What do you think of when you hear the word 'coin'? Money! Coin cards represent the material things in our lives. Our careers, our homes, our finances, our belongings. Because Coins represent the physical things we have in life, they are associated with Earth signs Virgo, Capricorn and Taurus, who are down to earth, stubborn, grounded and organized. When out of balance these cards can signify instability, conflict, financial frustration, spiritual dissatisfaction, vanity and lethargy with work matters. These cards can also represent some of the opportunities or blockages that you might face in these areas. They may also suggest some of the people that will share this journey or experience with you and who will either help or hinder you.

× **KEY WORDS** ×
Earth signs · Stability · Finances · Career · Home
Family · Grounded

MEMORIZING THE CARDS

If you want to try to solidify the meanings of the cards so that you do not always have to refer to a guide, start with one word for each suit – 'passion' for Wands, 'mentality' for Swords, 'emotions' for Cups and 'the material' for Coins. You can also practise by pulling a random card and testing to see if you can remember which area it represents. Practice really does make perfect, and this is exactly how I memorized all the card meanings. With enough repetition, you will instinctively know which area of your life needs attention by looking at how many of each suit you have pulled!

MEASURING TIME WITH TAROT

As much as I recommend against hyper-fixating on the timings of things, the suits can also be used to measure time. Here's what they stand for, together with an easy way to memorize each of them:

WANDS Represent Days
(Wands = wishes = instantaneous)

SWORDS Represent Weeks
(Swords = intellect = quick)

CUPS Represent Months
(Cups = emotional investment = months)

COINS Represent Years
(Coins = stability = years)

Although you can use tarot to measure time, it is important to remember not to get too wrapped up in this aspect of a reading. Remember that we have free will and can alter our path at any moment. Sometimes there is a waiting process where other things need to fall into place and timings can remain unclear. It is best to focus on the process that is needed rather than specific timings as a way to work through a given situation.

CHOOSING THE RIGHT DECK FOR YOU

When buying your first tarot deck, it is important to choose one that has traditional imagery, such as the Rider Waite deck or any deck inspired by it. This clear imagery will make it so much easier to interpret the cards, as much insight can be gained from the details. For example, the expression on a character's face, what they are facing toward or away from, the kind of environment they are in, whether a scene is calm or aggressive, and whether other figures feature on the card. Any tarot deck based on the Rider Waite imagery will have all the visual details needed to give an accurate reading. The illustrations are loaded with symbolism to help you interpret their meanings. Even if the imagery is marginally different in each Rider Waite inspired deck, the overall meaning of each card remains the same. The artist for the illustrations in this book has created a beautiful, modernized version of the cards using classic Rider Waite imagery so that you can easily decipher the symbolism.

Although this guide includes everything you need to know about each of the card's meanings, it is a good idea

The Nine of Swords represents mental anguish, worry, stress, sleeplessness, dread, anxiety and overwhelm, all of which are depicted in the card's traditional imagery.

to buy a deck that comes with a pamphlet that lists key words for each card. As meanings vary slightly with different decks, the pamphlet may contain extra information that relates specifically to that deck.

Buy your tarot deck in person if you can. There is a common myth that you must have your first tarot deck bestowed upon you as a gift and that you cannot purchase one for yourself, but it is not bad luck to buy your own tarot deck. It is not an issue if you are gifted your first deck, either. If you believe in divine timing, this might be a fortuitous introduction to tarot.

Buying in person means you can look through the cards and you will almost certainly feel drawn more towards one deck than another. It allows you to make sure the imagery is clear and to see that the deck feels comfortable in your hands and that you like the general overall feel of the deck. Tarot reading is a self-care exercise, and you want to enjoy the process.

SETTING UP YOUR ENVIRONMENT

When reading tarot cards, it is important to do so in an environment that is both comfortable and private. You need to focus and remain in tune with yourself so be sure to find a quiet space in which you will be free from interruptions.

CLEANSING THE SPACE

Have you ever walked into a room thick with atmosphere after an argument between two people? It is important not to have old energy lingering around the cards before you commence a reading, so cleanse your space by opening a window.

If you would like to delve deeper into the spiritual element of tarot practice, you can burn incense or candles. Simply light one end of an incense stick and allow the smoke to drift over the cards and around the area. Incense has the added benefit of aromatherapy and there are many scents available, such as lavender for relaxation and peppermint to reduce stress. If you prefer not to use incense, light a candle and hover your cards over the flame to cleanse them (obviously avoiding direct contact with the flame).

A CLEANSING VISUALIZATION

Sit in a comfortable position with your spine straight and with the cards resting gently in your hands. Close your eyes and start to tune into your natural breathing pattern. Take a few deep breaths through your nose, slowly inhaling for several seconds, holding briefly, and then gently exhaling. As you settle into this breathing pattern, start to envision a bright white light growing and expanding at your centre with each inhale and exhale. For the final few breaths, envision that bright white light flowing out from you, moving over the cards and throughout the space of your reading. If you are not into the visualization, just doing the breathing element of the exercise will help you feel more grounded, centred and ready to digest the reading ahead of you.

NUMEROLOGY IN TAROT READINGS

Each tarot card has its own corresponding number. The cards in the Major Arcana are numbered from 0 to 21. Those in the Minor Arcana are numbered from ace (one) to ten with an additional Page, Knight, Queen and King in each set. Each number has its own unique meaning, and this can help to give you a deeper understanding of the situations you are facing and the phases of a cycle you are currently going through (or are stuck in).

✦ Low numbers such as zero or one represent being in the early stages of a cycle.

✦ High numbers such as nine or ten represent finalizing or completing a process.

✦ A Page, Knight, Queen and King also increase in experience as you progress from Page to King. A Page represents student energy, a Knight represents action and being in motion, a Queen represents leadership potential, and a King represents authority potential.

WHAT DOES EACH NUMBER MEAN?

Memorizing just one of the following meanings for each number will help you to read the cards more easily.

ACE: Beginnings, fresh starts, doorways, offers, news
TWO: Options, choices, decisions
THREE: Collaborations, groups, growth, expansion, development, projects
FOUR: Stability, security, consolation, order
FIVE: Change, need for change, friction, power struggles, taking control, relationships, chaotic passions
SIX: Harmony, giving and receiving, transition period, departure, presence, acceptance, parting
SEVEN: Choices, making a stand, taking action, commitment, growth
EIGHT: Boundaries, ideas, change, news, karma, strength, success, expression
NINE: Culmination, nearing an end, reflection, gratitude, lessons, knowledge, wisdom, effort
TEN: Completion, results, culmination, fulfilment
PAGE: Youth, service, learning, student, beginnings, devotion
KNIGHT: Passion, action, drive, ambition, impulse, mobility
QUEEN: Leadership, management, teacher, wisdom, commitment
KING: Authority figures, stability, power, grounded, maturity

PUTTING THE BASICS TOGETHER

Now that you have some knowledge about the different suits and numbers and what they mean, you can start putting them together to interpret the cards. The following examples should give you the idea for how to do this.

ACE OF WANDS

We know that Aces represent beginnings and that Wands signify passion. This suggests that you could benefit from exploring a passionate new beginning! Aces hint at brief moments that need to be seized and so this card has a very 'seize the moment' energy. Look at the imagery – the hand is reaching for/grabbing this opportunity! If you have asked about a specific topic, this will relate directly to it. For example:

✦ If it is a love reading, the card probably represents an exciting and passionate new connection coming in, or aims to get your spark to return to a current one.

✦ If you have asked for a career reading, this hints at a very exhilarating new career prospect/pathway!

✦ If you are currently struggling with motivation or are feeling stressed out, this card suggests that you can find inspiration by exploring new ideas or environments.

TWO OF COINS

We know that twos signify choices and that Coins represent career, finances and home. This suggests that you could benefit from making an important change with regard to your work/life balance. The imagery shows a man juggling – it is therefore asking you to consider if you are juggling your responsibilities or if you are spreading yourself too thin. A decision may need to be made in order to find balance. If you have asked about a specific topic, this will relate directly to it. For example:

✦ In a love-focused reading, this card could suggest needing to choose between two connections or maybe even between your partner and your job. A decision needs to be made so that priorities are made clear, and progress can be made.

✦ In a career reading, the card suggests making a choice between two different opportunities. If you do not decide soon you could face consequences that negatively impact both.

NINE OF WANDS

Nines signify nearing completion and Wands represent goals/ambition. This suggests you are nearing the end of a project. The imagery shows a man looking backwards – a reminder to reflect on how far you have already come in the pursuit of your goals and to keep pushing forwards. If you have asked about a specific topic, this will relate directly to it. For example:

✦ In a love reading, the card suggests that you keep pushing forwards in a relationship. If you are single, it may suggest you stay focused on your current goals for now, but love may be an option around the corner.

✦ In a career reading, the card hints at perseverance. You may be exhausted by your attempts to finish a project but it would be a waste of your time and energy to give up now!

INTERACTION BETWEEN CARDS

Tarot can reveal a lot of information if you know how to look for it. For example, cards that feature people can be read in different ways depending on the direction they are facing. When a figure on a card is turned away from the imagery on the card beside it, this could signify that you are potentially ignoring or neglecting whatever that imagery represents. If the figure is facing towards the imagery, this could mean whatever it represents has your full attention. The direction in which a figure is facing can highlight your current priorities or something that is commancing your attention.

Ask yourself these questions: How does the person on the card feel? What are they doing? What colours are there? What climate is it? Do any symbols or numbers stick out? Are they looking towards or away from something? Consider the examples on the following pages.

In this positioning, two kings sit at ease facing one another. They both appear relaxed, engaged with each other and enjoying a stimulating conversation. If this arrangement came through in your reading, it would represent somebody you can trust, learn from, who views you as an equal and wants to help you succeed. You may benefit from the qualities or perspective of the other individual coming through.

In this positioning, the King of Wands is not really interested in what the King of Cups has to say, suggesting that you might be better off investing your time and energy elsewhere.

Here, the King of Wands interacts with the Knight of Coins – perhaps the Knight has brought some news. The King of Cups is not involved. Since Cups represent the emotions, this positioning suggests you are neglecting an emotional outlook on the situation and prioritizing finances instead.

With these cards, it appears that the Seven of Swords is assisting the Knight of Swords in some kind of venture. They are both moving in the same direction and are equipped with swords for whatever challenge lays ahead.

With the cards swapping places, it appears the Seven of Swords has been up to some mischief, sneaking around and stealing, and that the Knight of Swords is pursuing them in the name of justice. In a reading, this might suggest any doubts you have about a situation or person could do with further investigation. These cards invite you to be valiant in your efforts (like the Knight of Swords) and not to be afraid but stand up for/defend yourself.

BEGINNER TAROT SPREADS

Using spreads is a great tool for receiving clearer messages as they allow you to distinguish what each card is representing. A spread gives you more context, enabling you to break down a situation and see what is happening. The most common go-to spread for any tarot reader is the classic Celtic Cross spread, but I have also created spreads for self-empowerment, self-care and relationships as well.

CELTIC CROSS SPREAD

Shuffle the deck, then select and place the cards one by one, matching the pattern opposite. Each card represents its corresponding number. The Celtic Cross spread is fantastic if you want overall advice about where you currently are and how things are going to pan out. It helps bring clarity to what has happened, looks at the current influences on your life and offers approaches to moving forwards. It is a fantastic all-round and in-depth spread that you can use for yourself and others in any situation.

1 Your current energy
2 Opportunity/challenge
3 What to focus on
4 Recent past
5 Strengths
6 Near future
7 Suggested approach
8 Environmental factors
9 Hopes and fears
10 Final outcome

BEGINNER TAROT SPREADS

SELF-EMPOWERMENT SPREAD

This is a twist on the classic past/present/future spread. It will give you clarity and insight into your recent experiences, let you know what needs your attention right now and also provides helpful suggestions for approaches to take. A key part of being empowered is being able to accept and release the past, to increase your self-awareness and to make sure that you are well equipped for what lies ahead. This spread encapsulates each aspect of this and will lead you to the ultimate self-empowerment!

SELF-CARE SPREAD

This fantastic self-care spread is made of three parts for the ultimate check in. Part one (cards one to three) reveals which parts of yourself are you paying attention to and which parts are you neglecting; part two (cards four to five) shows how you currently perceive yourself and how this is affecting your trajectory; and part three (card six) shows the heights you could reach if you truly allowed yourself to go for it.

1 Mental state
2 Physical state
3 Spiritual state
4 Current perception of self
5 Current direction
6 Heights you could reach

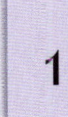  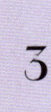

INTERACTIONS WITH OTHERS SPREAD

Use this spread to examine connections in your life – romantic partners, family members, friends or business partners. It will reveal each person's intentions, any difficulties that you may need to overcome together and what this is leading you towards. You will notice the spread has two trajectories, labelled as 'current' and 'potential'. This is a reminder that you can change your reality with the choices you make. This spread will show you if the challenges you face are possible to overcome or if they are insurmountable and you need to invest your energy elsewhere.

1 What are their desires/intentions?
2 What are your desires/intentions?
3 Their current energy
4 Your current energy
5 Their blockages/challenges
6 Your blockages/challenges
7 Current trajectory
8 Potential trajectory
9 Best action moving forwards

TIPS FOR READING SPREADS

✦ Plan to take breaks. Do not repeatedly look at the same situation over and over again. You want to avoid any kind of obsessive reading of the same situation.

✦ Take time to rest between readings and allow things to unfold naturally. Sometimes this can take days, weeks or even months. Sometimes there are hidden factors that you do not need to know about just yet.

✦ As best as you can, try to read the cards with an objective point of view. It can be easy to try to see what you want to see and overlook the things you do not want to believe about yourself or someone else.

✦ If a seemingly negative message does come through for you, do not panic. Using any of the spreads included in this guide, along with the card meanings that follow, the cards will identify what needs your attention and what the best course of action will be moving forwards. You will always have something to work on. Try your best to focus on the things you can control while allowing everything else to unfold naturally.

✦ If you do a heavy reading make sure to cleanse your space (and even yourself) as soon as the session is over. You can do this using incense, candles, a visualization, a shower, exercise or meditation. Keep the windows open, if you can, to let the energy disperse.

✦ Remember that practice makes perfect. Practise on yourself or practise with your friends and family members. You can also practise by doing a daily card pull in the morning to see what you need to keep in mind throughout the day.

The sections that follow look at what each tarot card actually means and how you can use this to self-reflect and become more empowered in your journey. Before diving into the meanings of the cards, remember that all of the approaches described above will help you to identify those areas of your life that need your attention and how far along each process you are. Use the following section to refer to when pulling cards for yourself and head into the future knowing that you have asked for all the tools needed to create the best out of each situation. Feel prepared. Feel empowered.

THE
MAJOR
ARCANA

The cards in the **Major Arcana** represent the major events, lessons and individuals we connect with. If multiple Major Arcana cards appear in a reading, it is likely you are experiencing a particularly transformational period of your life. As mentioned previously, each tarot card has a corresponding number. The 22 Major Arcana cards are numbered from **0 to 21**. Remember, the higher the number, the further along the development process you are. You can refer to the numerology table in the introduction if you would like to gain a little extra insight on this.

0
The Fool

KEY WORDS
Fresh start · Adventure · Opportunity · Excitement · Optimism
Self-discovery · Fulfilment

CARD MEANING

The Fool serves as a reminder to remain open to fresh starts, new adventures and unforeseen opportunities. It represents stepping outside of the norm for the sake of your own self-discovery. Perhaps you are in the earliest 'idea' phase of a journey, yet to take a leap of faith.

The Fool can be inexperienced (like many embarking on a new pathway) and this card suggests that you should seek advice and/or listen to any counsel that is offered to you by those with more experience or who are loyal to your best interests (such as family members or close friends who want to look out for you).

Although you may be inexperienced, this card is also a reminder that you should not allow yourself to be too easily swayed by others, but to connect with and follow your own inner instincts. If you are thinking about taking things in a new direction, be sure to honour your own intuition while also being open to any guidance that is offered to you from those you trust. If you have a funny feeling about something

– for example, you feel someone might be trying to take advantage of you – try not to sweep this feeling aside and talk to someone you trust.

We often find ourselves drawn towards specific things in life for a reason, but it is important that you do not get too carried away and rush into making a decision without thinking things through properly first. Take time to consider the long-term implications of a decision or journey.

IMAGERY

The Fool is depicted as a young person gazing off into the distance, almost completely oblivious to the cliff edge right under their nose. This is a reminder that you can lack environmental awareness when in unfamiliar territory, and that you need to survey your surroundings or think about the long-term implications of your decisions before jumping into anything too quickly. The Fool's festive and youthful appearance suggests that you may have an enthusiastic approach to a new beginning or exciting adventure, but you should be realistic about any experience you have in this area and whether or not you need guidance. The youthful imagery is also a reminder of how much you have to gain or learn from a new and unfamiliar experience (like a young student).

The bag slung across The Fool's shoulder hints at some kind of last-minute or spontaneous adventure. Therefore, a degree of anticipation and excitement will be fuelling you when it comes to making this exciting new decision.

The bag's small size suggests either unpreparedness or minimalism. You will benefit from getting things in order so that you can be more prepared, but also so that you are not weighed down too much by baggage.

The white rose in The Fool's hand is a symbol of having pure intentions and a reminder for you to keep these intentions in mind moving forwards. As long as your intentions are pure, you can rest assured that you are moving in the right direction and that you will reap the rewards of this new venture.

The mountains in the background hint at the bigger picture and future obstacles that may not be in your current awareness but probably need to be taken into consideration.

The Fool's small, white companion dog embodies the need to seek advice from someone who is loyal to your best interests.

The sun in the top-right corner of the card symbolizes the optimism and joy that can be found from taking things in a new direction.

The red feather on The Fool's head is a symbol of a new idea/breakthrough that will begin a new cycle for you.

1
The Magician

KEY WORDS
Manifestation · Untapped potential · Creativity · Willpower
Discipline · Imagination · Self-confidence

CARD MEANING

The Magician represents the different elements that are important in the early stages of a creative process. It asks that you reflect on any untapped potential and consider whether there is something exciting or potentially fruitful that you have not allowed yourself to explore yet.

This card serves as a reminder that you already have the necessary tools to create the life, career or relationship you want for yourself, but that you must both believe something is possible and take action towards it in order for it to become your reality. When you combine these two elements (belief and action) you are able to step into your full potential.

Known as the 'manifestation' card, whenever The Magician appears in a reading, you must establish a clear vision of what you want to accomplish and why. Ask yourself how your day-to-day life would look if you achieved this goal. Allow yourself to envision this reality in your mind's eye: What do you see? What do you feel? Where are you and who are you with?

Write all the details down if you can to solidify them further.

This card suggests that it is more important to take things one step at a time than to expect yourself to achieve everything in one go. Limit your distractions and use the knowledge, skills and wisdom you have already gained in order to help guide you towards this new goal.

It is time to tap into your creativity!

IMAGERY

See how The Magician has one hand pointing towards the sky and the other pointing down towards Earth. This represents the importance of having a balanced connection to both your spiritual and material goals.

On the table in front of The Magician are objects representing the four tarot suits: a wand, a sword, a cup and a coin. They suggest that you already have everything you need to manifest the reality you want for yourself: the passion, the intellect, the emotional desire and a material connection.

The red and yellow colours remind you to remain optimistic and to fully honour your own power/potential by choosing to believe in yourself.

The flowers and shrubbery in the foreground represent your own ability to manifest abundance into your life and to bring these goals to fruition if you apply yourself and decide to believe in yourself.

An infinity symbol hovers above The Magician's head and a snake eating its own tail is wrapped around their body. Both represent limitless potential. Perhaps you are sitting on untapped potential – what do you have to share with the world that you have been holding yourself back from?

2
The High Priestess

KEY WORDS
Intuition · Personal exploration · Conscious and subconscious
A quiet and deep inner knowing · Concealment · Secrets

CARD MEANING

When The High Priestess appears in a reading, it suggests that you should explore something for yourself before deciding to trust someone else wholeheartedly. Sometimes you must look beyond the information that is being shown to you. Do not be afraid to trust your own intuition. This card also highlights the benefits of exploring any subconscious influences that might be affecting or altering your experience.

The High Priestess suggests that not every situation is quite as it appears on the surface. People are not always genuine or honest. Sometimes they opt not to share important details with you.

Because this card is associated with strong intuition and instincts, you are being urged to connect with these. It can be a good exercise to write: 'What is my intuition telling me that I am ignoring?' List anything that comes to mind – there are no right or wrong answers. It offers an opportunity to make your own personal exploration of something as a way of finding out more information.

THE HIGH PRIESTESS

The High Priestess can represent hidden secrets and a chance for you to dive into your own spiritual evolution. Those who are brave enough to listen to their inner insight will find greater strength and conviction.

You are being asked to trust your own personal experience and to make sure that you are not allowing anyone else to deceive you. Do some digging before committing yourself to something/someone. Anything that feels 'off' most likely is.

IMAGERY

The High Priestess sits peacefully in her temple. Clearly religious, spiritual and intuitive, she serves as a reminder for you to connect with those aspects within yourself.

The white cross around her neck is a symbol of integrity and honour and signifies the importance of purity and truth.

The veil hanging behind The High Priestess represents the separation between the seen and the unseen. What is being shown to you may not be fully accurate; something might be hidden from your view. This can also represent the division between the conscious and the unconscious mind.

The pomegranates on the veil are associated with the Greek goddess Persephone and represent divine feminine energy. Do not be afraid to try to engage with your own intuition and emotions to help you figure out what is really going on behind closed doors, or how something is affecting you.

This might lead to you learning more about yourself or somebody/something else.

The partly concealed scroll in her lap suggests you may not have all the information needed just yet and that further exploration or inquiry may be needed.

The crescent moon by her feet is another symbol of intuition, but also hints at something that is not showing in its entirety. Remember to keep a bigger picture in mind!

3
The Empress

KEY WORDS
Divine feminine power · Mother Earth · Creation · Patient nurturing
Growth · Development · Action

CARD MEANING

The Empress card portrays a woman who is focusing on watering her garden with care and patience. She sits comfortable in the knowledge that as long as she carefully tends to her plants, she will reap the rewards of the harvest. The card is a reminder that where your attention goes, energy flows, and that it is time to focus on your own development and growth rather than getting distracted by other people's projects, goals or appearances.

This card is connected to the Greek goddess Venus and can be a reminder to honour the divine feminine. This may relate to a connection in your life such as a partner, friend or family member or it could be a signal to connect with your own divine femininity.

This card is known as the Mother Earth archetype. When it appears in a reading, you are being encouraged to connect more with the natural world around you. Spend more time outdoors in direct connection to the elements – in a garden,

a forest or near a natural body of water, for example. You will gain fresh insight by allowing yourself to reconnect with Mother Earth and by appreciating the different cycles she goes through. The card also asks you to honour the cycles we go through in life – life and death, rest and action, creation and destruction. It is a reminder that one cannot exist without the other and opposing aspects need to be acknowledged and appreciated during a creation process.

This card can also symbolize pregnancy or birth and, more generally, the birthing of a new idea or process. In order for something to grow, you must give it the right conditions. It is time to prioritize your own growth.

IMAGERY

See how The Empress sits on a luxurious throne in the middle of a lush, fertile garden. This represents the importance of watering your own garden instead of comparing yourself to others or prioritizing their agenda above your own. Her soft feminine features serve as a reminder to approach things with care and compassion. Do not expect too much from yourself and do not try to force anything either. Be patient with the process.

The pomegranates on the The Empress's dress are a symbol of the divine feminine, fertility and abundance.

The nature that surrounds her suggests there is a time for growth and a time for rest.

The abundance of greenery symbolizes the potential of what you could accomplish if you decided to invest your time, energy and effort in your own endeavours.

The crown of stars on her head serves as a reminder to connect with the spiritual realm and your spiritual goals.

The 12 stars on the crown represent the natural cycles in life – for example, the 12 months of the year, the 12 signs of the Western zodiac. They signify that spiritual and material aspects must be balanced in order to find sustainability moving forward.

4
The Emperor

KEY WORDS
Confidence · Skilful execution · Foresight · Control and coordination
Leadership · Wisdom · Chivalry

CARD MEANING

When The Emperor card appears in a reading, it is a sign that you could benefit from stepping up into a more leadership-focused role. Whether this involves acting as a father figure (regardless of gender), a leader or more self-governing, you are being asked to put yourself in a position where you have the opportunity to navigate greater challenges and to protect and guide others.

The card shows great potential for embracing a high-pressure environment in which other people look up to you for guidance and wisdom. It is a sign that your willingness to take control of the situation and to show confidence in your own abilities (or maybe even learn directly from someone else who has these qualities) will ultimately lead to your growth. But the card is also a reminder that grand achievements are not always built overnight and that they require a period of dedication, foresight and hard work. It highlights the importance of being strategic and organized in your approach to work or other matters and asks you to use your

intelligence and wisdom to create more structure so that you can find the calm within the chaos.

Be sure to get a plan in place as this will make you more likely to follow it through to the end. Anyone who receives this card in a reading has great potential for being a boss, father, teacher, mentor or even just a good friend. Do not underestimate the value you bring to the table.

The card can sometimes suggest that you need to respect and learn from an authority figure in your life such as a father, boss or friend; whether it is representing you or someone else will be determined by your choice of spread.

IMAGERY

The Emperor clearly depicts somebody in a position of power. Sitting confidently and upright on their throne, they naturally command attention and respect from those around them. The stern face shows that matters should always be taken seriously and with a lot of consideration if you want their outcome to be long-lasting and sustainable. Ask yourself whether you have something to gain by showing more confidence in your own abilities. Do you have something to learn from someone in a position of power?

The Emperor's white beard is symbolic of the knowledge and wisdom you have gained on your own journey. It may also hint at someone who has an abundance of wisdom and experience to share with you.

The Emperor's crown suggests that success and influence can be (or have been) gained from a period of dedication, hard work and commitment.

The mountains in the background represent stability and symbolize how important it is to be 'grounded' and 'secure' in yourself and your goals. Do you know what you are working towards and why?

The colour red symbolizes the raw power and potential that can come from embracing the qualities of The Emperor.

5
The Hierophant

KEY WORDS
Tradition · Commitment · Integrity · Alliance · Learning
Practice · Assurance

CARD MEANING

The Hierophant card appears in a reading as a reminder that, regardless of how well established you are, you are sometimes in need of guidance and can benefit from a teacher, mentor or authority figure to help show you how to commit to something in a more structured and efficient way.

This card represents a period of dedication or study that must happen before you can continue down a pathway on your own accord. It suggests that you have much to gain from those who have greater knowledge in the area you hope to explore. This card might come through with The Fool card; when it does, it represents the teacher rather than the student.

The Hierophant is a card of tradition and so you will most likely benefit from committing to tried-and-true methods rather than using those that are innovative or risky. This card can also hint at spiritual, religious or self-care practices that have been neglected or abandoned and the need to re-commit yourself to some of these.

This card can represent a group or institution that has well established beliefs/methods that are known for being successful, and symbolizes the comfort and stability that can be found from that. It could relate to a religious group, support group, family dynamic or specialist led class, for example.

As there are several spiritual elements associated with this card, it is also asking you to keep your values in mind while pursuing something. Ask yourself if your words/intentions are in alignment with your actions. Are you living your truth and doing what you say you are going to do? Do you need to enrol in a course to get a better base knowledge of something? Could you benefit from the guidance of somebody who has more experience?

IMAGERY

The individuals at the bottom of the image look up to this religious figure for support and guidance. They serve as a reminder that you may also benefit from having a mentor or somebody with an abundance of information in an area you would like to explore or develop in.

The followers awaiting instruction from The Hierophant suggest that an initiation process or rite of passage needs to be gained in order for you to take things to the next level. You may be waiting for approval on something, or you may even need to gain more knowledge about something before you can go out on your own.

The two keys crossed at The Hierophant's feet represent the fact that this person or institution is the only one that can help you unlock the next chapter.

As the religious symbology is a sign of commitment, ask if you are committing yourself to living a life in alignment with your value system. Are your words and actions lining up? Are you living your truth? Are you doing what you say you are going to do?

6
The Lovers

KEY WORDS

Decision-making · Honouring your spiritual, emotional and physical needs · Following your heart · Fearlessness · Vulnerability

---

CARD MEANING

When The Lovers card appears in a reading, it is a reminder that your physical, emotional and spiritual aspects all need to be taken into consideration when making an important decision (especially concerning a relationship).

This card can represent a very strong attraction towards something or someone and can also hint at the things in life that physically tempt us. It is a reminder that your emotional and spiritual needs still need to be implemented despite these physical desires/urges. If you want to experience the depth of love that you desire and deserve then you will need to be willing to be true to yourself and own these emotional/spiritual needs.

The nakedness on this card is symbolic of the vulnerability involved in putting your whole self forward and represents your willingness to embrace raw honesty and open communication. This card asks that you stay true to who you are by being fully authentic with the people around you, especially your loved ones.

When faced with confusion in a situation, it is always best to put your best/true self forward and act in alignment with your beliefs and values. The Lovers card represents the choices you must make in your life that are not always about the most convenience or ease but that will actually honour your needs and values.

As the two people on the card are mirroring each other, it is important to remember that opposites attract for a reason. Try to look at what learning can be gained from anyone who is mirroring something back to you.

IMAGERY

The card features a naked man and woman – their nakedness is a reminder of how integral vulnerability is in your close relationships. Notice how the man looks toward the woman and the woman looks up toward the spirit guide. This signifies the unconscious, conscious and super conscious or physical attraction, emotional needs and spiritual concerns. This is a reminder that all three aspects need to be considered when making a decision.

The tree of flames behind the man represents passionate desires and physical urges or attractions that can influence you at this time.

The apple tree with a serpent winding around it behind the woman represents temptation and how this can influence your decision-making.

The volcano in the background is a symbol of the explosion of potential that can come from honouring your physical, emotional and spiritual needs.

The spirit guide above the couple blesses their experience and is symbolic of the importance of having a connection to your higher self (or morals and ethics) when making decisions based on love.

7
The Chariot

KEY WORDS
Initiating change · Taking a stand · Overcoming adversity
Triumphing through obstacles · Remaining focused · Travel

CARD MEANING

The Chariot card reminds you that slow and steady progress in a clear direction is always more efficient than trying to do everything at once. You are being asked to implement the lessons you have learned from The Lovers card – to make decisions in alignment with your best self even when they are not the most easy or convenient course of action, and to trust your heart when your mind tries to convince you otherwise.

This card represents harnessing opposing forces (sometimes you want to do the work and sometimes you do not) and highlights the importance of willpower and discipline. We are all faced with distractions and challenges that test how serious we are about our goals, so this is a reminder to stay focused and stick to your current plan/path. Perseverance will get you further than constantly changing directions. This card suggests that you can be successful in your endeavours if you stay committed and disciplined.

If you are wondering if you have what it takes to accomplish something, The Chariot is a fantastic reminder that you can create this reality for yourself if you know who you are and what you stand for. This will help you to push past any obstacles that get in your way (this can include your own self-limiting beliefs).

The Chariot card is associated with movement and can sometimes represent a reminder for you to go and travel, to change your residence or to go on a voyage of some kind. Adventure will keep your spirit alive!

IMAGERY

This woman stands tall inside her chariot, reminding you to have confidence in yourself and to be certain in your decisions (even if you have to fake it until you make it). Notice how the reigns are loose, a sign that you do not need to 'force' anything or anyone to get what you want. Being confident in your vision and deciding to face obstacles as they appear is much more important than trying to control everything.

The woman wears a crown – a reminder to connect with the wisdom that you have already gained and implement this moving forward.

The crescent moons represent that you are still in the process of stepping into your full potential and there is so much more that you are capable of that you have not seen in action yet. This moon imagery is also a reminder to stay connected to your intuition.

The black and white sphinxes represent opposing forces, black and white, day and night, and are a reminder that one thing cannot exist without the other. As Carl Jung once said: 'No tree can reach to heaven if its roots do not reach down to hell.'

The river in the background suggests that, sometimes, you need to go with the flow.

8
Strength

KEY WORDS
Courage · Self-discipline · Harnessing energy · Determination
Honouring your own diversity

CARD MEANING

The Strength card comes through as a reminder that you do not always have to be the loudest or strongest person in the room in order to have the most success or influence.

This card highlights the impact you can create on your life – and on the lives of others – by using discipline and willpower. It is a reminder that we all have peaceful and fiery qualities within us, and that you should harness both of these energies to have a balanced and sustainable approach moving forward. Allow the fire in your belly to guide you towards the things you are passionate about and at the same time be disciplined and patient with your progress. This card hints at your inner strength and your ability to commit yourself.

Not everything in life is worthy of a reaction, and sometimes you have to fight some of your impulses to remain on higher ground. This card highlights the importance of composure and maturity and although you may sometimes find yourself feeling anger, disappointment, sadness or frustration, you are

being asked to search for a healthy outlet for these instead of lashing out and reacting easily. Make sure you have something healthy to invest that fiery energy in so that it does not overpower you. (Some examples of this are journalling, exercise, being goal driven).

Self-discipline is the key to self-mastery, and this is your reminder to honour all of these fiery aspects so that you can become more confident in your own abilities. Figuring out how to channel this passionate energy into the correct avenues, will enable you to become more efficient in your endeavours.

This card can also signify the benefits of being able to influence others without it being immediately apparent to yourself or everyone else. (Once again, a reminder that you don't have to be the loudest in the room to have the most influence).

IMAGERY

This image is of a woman caressing a lion, an animal known for its ferocity and power, and yet somehow she is able to tame it and get it to listen to her. See how nurturing she is – a sign that she does not have to coerce or force the lion to do anything and a reminder that your own animalistic qualities can be channelled into passion and productivity.

The woman's white dress is symbolic of your own purity, innocence and the importance of having good intentions when influencing others.

The belt of flowers around her waist and on her head represent the abundance and success that can be found from having both a compassionate yet disciplined approach.

The infinity symbol above her head serves to remind you of your limitless potential.

The lion gazing up at her is a reminder of your own ability to influence and guide others.

9
The Hermit

KEY WORDS
Reflection · Solitude · Inner exploration · Reassessment
Shadow work · Finding clarity

CARD MEANING

The Hermit card represents somebody who has embarked on a significant journey of self-discovery. It represents the period of intense self-reflection and growth that can come from spending more distraction-free time with yourself. This card is an invitation to retreat into your own private world and to allow your inner wisdom to guide you, instead of constantly distracting yourself with work, stress, your phone or TV.

This card is a reminder that, sometimes, we need to reassess our direction and that we can find the answers we need by searching within ourselves. Connecting with yourself can sometimes feel like a time of darkness or isolation yet it is during this time of solitude that the most important things become illuminated.

This card is symbolic of the many benefits of shadow work and suggests that it can help you to overpower subconscious influences that may be impacting you from past experiences. Anyone who is brave enough to dive into this intense period

of self-discovery will emerge with powerful realizations or breakthroughs. You hold all the answers – now is the time to seek them out by limiting your distractions and connecting with your own inner voice.

IMAGERY

See how this woman stands alone at the top of a mountain peak – a sign of the long journey you have been on and all of the spiritual lessons you have learned along the way.

The Hermit holds up a lantern with a six-pointed star. It is symbolic of the wisdom you have already gained and how this can help to illuminate the next steps required from you. Notice how dim the lantern is, a reminder that even if you can only see a little way ahead of you, taking those first few steps will allow the following steps to become clearer.

The staff she holds in her other hand hints at your own authority and shows you that you can lean on yourself for support.

10
The Wheel of Fortune

KEY WORDS

Unexpected change · Going with the flow · Unforeseen joy
Good karma · Forward movement/momentum

CARD MEANING

When The Wheel of Fortune appears in a reading, it is a reminder that many things are outside of your control, and sometimes it is much better to move with the flow than it is to resist it. Have you ever heard how the bamboo plant bends with the wind, so it does not break? Try to remember this when you feel yourself resisting any unexpected changes that crop up in your life.

If you are somebody that likes to hold on to control, you may find unpredictability extra challenging. However, you should trust that whatever you are being redirected towards can always be in alignment with your best interests if you allow yourself to be open to the experience.

Sometimes unexpected changes can make you feel as if things are falling apart. But what if oversleeping sees you avoiding a major road accident? You might spill coffee on

yourself and bump into someone incredibly important in the bathroom while cleaning yourself up. Sometimes you are denied something good because you deserve something much greater. Do not forget that blessings can be hidden in disguise.

This card also urges you to enjoy something before it is too late. It serves as a reminder to put your best (and most patient) self forward in all situations so that you do not have any regrets. Life can be unpredictable but take the changes for what they are, without too much judgment.

The Wheel of Fortune is also symbolic of karma – what goes around comes around. If you have been making decisions in alignment with your highest self, you can rest assured that there will be unforeseen joy ahead.

IMAGERY

The card shows a giant wheel, a symbol of movement, change and unstoppable momentum. The remaining imagery on the card is chaotic and symbolizes the many different aspects that are in play at all times and how unpredictable life can be.

There is a sign of the Western zodiac in each corner:
Aquarius, Scorpio, Taurus and Leo. Each of these is a fixed star sign and serves as a reminder to focus on the things in your life that bring you stability when you are going through unexpected changes.

The Egyptian god Anubis is bottom right of the wheel. He represents life and death, creation and destruction and how one cannot exist without the other. In order for one cycle to start another must end and this is sometimes the only way you can progress forwards in life.

The sphinx sitting on top of the wheel represents your knowledge, wisdom and ability to rise above change and find stability and calm amid the chaos.

The snake descending on the left-hand side hints at your connection to the material world and the physical/material changes you experience in life.

11
Justice

KEY WORDS
Fairness · Levelheadedness · Responsibility
Accountability · Objectivity

CARD MEANING

The Justice card represents any matter relating to fairness. When this card comes through, it signifies that someone needs to be called to account for their actions. If you or they have been living in alignment with your spiritual values, you have nothing to worry about. The card also serves as a reminder of the importance of compassion and that we should judge others fairly and without bias.

This card might come through in a legal situation, in which case it suggests a final verdict or firm decision is going to be made. If you are seeking justice for yourself, this card is normally a good sign. If you have done something you regret, you can trust that you will be judged fairly.

This card can also appear when you are about to make a significant decision and need to consider the long-term implications of your actions. It is important to balance both logic and intuition when making a decision, especially if the outcome is likely to affect someone else. You need to be able to stand by your decisions and accept the consequences.

To put it simply, this is a card of karma, cause and effect, and fair judgment. It highlights the importance of taking full responsibility and accountability for your decisions and actions. Make sure that you are acting in alignment with your highest self and judge others fairly. Some things are not always as black and white as they seem. Be compassionate with yourself and others.

IMAGERY

See how this woman sits between two pillars, representing balance, law and structure. In her right hand she holds an upright sword and in her left a pair of scales.

The sword that she holds represents your mental aspects. It is a sign of needing to use intellect, but is also a reminder that your actions carry consequences (double-edged sword). The sword pointing upwards signifies that a firm decision needs to be made.

The scales suggest you need to balance your intuition and your logic and make sure that both of these are being taken into account when a decision is made. If this card represents someone else, you can trust that you are going to get a fair and well-balanced judgment.

The square on Justice's crown represents the importance of having well-ordered thoughts when making decisions.

A small white shoe pokes out of her robes – a reminder of the spiritual consequences of your actions and the importance of having pure intentions.

A purple veil hangs in the background. It is a colour of compassion and represents your need to consider that.

12
The Hanged Man

KEY WORDS
Ultimate surrender · Sacrifice · Enlightenment
Perspective · Reflection

CARD MEANING

The Hanged Man invites you to pause briefly and examine things from a new perspective. If you continue to look at a situation from just one viewpoint, you may find yourself stuck in an unhelpful pattern of behaviour or miss out on important information that could help you see the bigger picture.

Although your world may sometimes be flipped upside down, it is from this new, uncomfortable position that you will find alternative perspectives and experience significant personal breakthroughs. This very pivotal card in tarot represents some of the more major life lessons and shifts of perspective that can stay with you for the rest of your life because your world was flipped upside down. It is a card of ultimate surrender and a sign of the peace/enlightenment that you will gain from surrendering to new perspectives/positions. This card also highlights the importance of making sacrifices in order to find a solution.

Remember: if you always do what you have always done, you will always get what you have always got. This card is a calling for you to let go of old perspectives or patterns of behaviour and belief systems as a way to move up to the next level. Your sacrifice will be rewarded with clarity, and you will be living more in alignment with your highest self as a result.

IMAGERY

A woman hangs upside down with a calm and serene expression on her face. Her position hints at a huge shift of perspective taking place and presents you with an opportunity to reflect on things from a different point of view. The woman's calm facial expression is a sign that your willingness to see things from this new perspective will allow you to find peace, serenity and surrender.

The light glowing around the woman's head is a sign of the new insights, awareness or spiritual enlightenments that come from embracing a shift in perspective.

The red of the woman's shorts symbolizes passion, whereas the blue of the woman's top symbolizes knowledge and wisdom. This imagery represents integrating these two aspects together to have a more balanced view on things.

The woman has a lot of skin on display. This represents an element of vulnerability that you may feel when being forced to view your life from a different standpoint.

13
Death

KEY WORDS

Foreseen endings · Transformation · Loss · Inevitability · Sacrifice
Purification · Acceptance

CARD MEANING

The Death card represents the unavoidable endings that we all must face in life. Depending on the circumstances, it could indicate a bereavement, the end of a significant relationship or letting go of a specific path you once envisioned for yourself.

This card is a sign that you need to be willing to let go of the things that are outside of your control. It is a reminder that you can use most (if not all) endings as an opportunity to transform your life. It normally signifies foreseen endings, so it is worth reflecting on whether this ending has come as a complete surprise to you. The card asks you to find peace in letting go and surrendering to a situation.

This card can also represent a period of mourning, so allow yourself time to come to terms with your loss. Acceptance takes time and it is important that you recognize that, in order to move forward, you must try to embrace the inevitable. Although some endings may be outside of your control, they can also bring unexpected joy and opportunity.

The Death card is not all bad. It can signify transformation, growth, new beginnings and rebirth. Even though some endings can be devastating, we can also find peace from accepting when something is over and by finding something more meaningful to invest in as a result.

IMAGERY

A skeleton wears a suit of armour. The skeleton is a reminder of what is left behind after an ending and the armour signifies that death is invincible – some endings cannot be avoided. Death is a part of life that we all must go through.

The skeleton holds a black flag with a white, five-petalled rose on it. The number five symbolizes change and the colour white symbolizes purity and spirituality. The rose represents the beauty that can still be found amid an upsetting ending.

The people in the foreground plead with and pray to the skeletal figure. One of them has her face turned away from the situation. This is a sign that you may feel tempted to beg for something (or someone) to be spared or that you might not want to face the reality of an ending. But this card is a reminder that death spares no one and you must accept that.

Two towers stand in the background, against a setting sun. This is a reminder that the sun sets and rises each day as a testament to endings and beginnings being intrinsically linked. This bright light can also be a symbol of the afterlife and a reminder of the joy and light that eventually comes after loss.

14
Temperance

KEY WORDS
Patience · Conscious moderation · Peaceful melding of opposites
Inner listening · Being accomodating

CARD MEANING

The appearance of Temperance in a reading serves as a reminder that sometimes you need to allow things to unfold without too much force or resistance. It suggests that keeping calm and collected will help you to respond to a situation accordingly.

This card asks you to honour the bigger picture (including other people's opinions and approaches that might not necessarily line up with your own) as a way to take a more balanced and well-rounded approach. It is also a reminder to honour what is needed rather than what your ego wants. This card suggests you should let go of trying to prove any kind of point or uphold any kind of appearance.

Not everything needs a reaction. Some situations are not as complicated as you make them and with a little reflection, you may be able to find a more appropriate solution for a problem you are facing. This card represents your ability to sit with discomfort and find middle ground. Your ability to

adapt will help you to create the best out of each situation. The Temperance card is also associated with alchemy so it can represent blended families, potential careers in mixology (blending alcohols), artistry (blending paints and colours) or even a chef (blending ingredients). This is a reminder that different elements must come together harmoniously to create the bigger picture.

IMAGERY

See how this woman pours water from one cup into another. This is a reminder to be contemplative, fluid and adaptable in your dealing with a situation. She has one foot on the land and the other under the water, suggesting that you will benefit from having a well-balanced approach to things. You can remain grounded while also being open to go with the flow. This imagery is also a reminder to balance your emotional and material pursuits.

The wings symbolize your connection to the spiritual realm and serve as a reminder to prioritize what your soul needs over what your ego wants. Remember to keep the bigger picture in mind and to consider other people's experiences even if it means you have to make some compromises. Do not forfeit the quality of your relationships simply to get what you want.

Temperance has a peaceful expression on her face – a reminder to try and stay calm amid the chaos and to take your time in considering things properly before jumping into a reaction.

The winding path behind her suggests that there is a bigger picture at play here and that there is a long path ahead of you and compromise/adjustment will be a huge factor in following that path.

15
The Devil

KEY WORDS
Desire · Indulgence · Undisciplined behaviour · Codependency
Urges · Temptation · Self-sabotage

CARD MEANING

When The Devil card appears in a reading, it is asking you to look at the different temptations in your life and to assess just how much these are governing you. Despite stereotypes, The Devil card is not an evil card. It represents the complex forces of desire, indulgence and abandonment that will either lead you to growth and freedom or bondage and addiction/enslavement.

When The Devil card comes up for you, you need to be extremely honest with yourself. Which forces are you currently allowing to govern you? Lust? Greed? Fear? Desire? Have any of these impulses led you away from your true self or from what you really want? This card represents a choice between indulgence and restraint and is often a sign that a new approach could be helpful.

Remember that you are an active creator of your experience, and identifying the ways in which you have been self-sabotaging will help you to move on from stagnant energy.

This card can be a sign of temptation for luxury items, sexual pleasure, financial gain or the avoidance of your emotions/responsibilities. It can also represent being in a codependent relationship. Keep in mind that you grow like the people you spend the most time with, so be mindful of the company you keep.

IMAGERY

A large creature that is half man, half goat features on this card, serving to remind us that we have both humanistic (tamed) and animalistic (wild) tendencies. The creature has vampire wings. Since vampires are known to suck life out of their victims, The Devil card asks you to look at relationships, environments or habits that take more energy from you than they to give in return.

The inverted pentagram on the creature's forehead is a symbol of dark, mystical energy and the potential of being distracted by temptations or urges.

The Devil has two prisoners. This symbolizes the things in your life that may currently have a hold over you and could be influencing your experience. Look closely, however. The chains around their necks are loose, signifying that you could escape from this hold or pattern of behaviour if you really wanted to. It is not too late.

The prisoners have horns on their heads, a sign that the longer you stay around certain energies the more likely you are to become like them. You are the company you keep.

The devil's tails on the prisoners are a reminder for you to look at the animalistic urges that may be influencing you – hunger, pleasure, shelter, and so on.

16
The Tower

KEY WORDS
Revelation · Destruction · Self-deception · Loss of security
Release in pressure · Coming back into balance

CARD MEANING

When The Tower card appears in a reading, you are being asked to reflect on whether you have tried to plant yourself somewhere unsustainable.

Sometimes unexpected devastation can be the universe's way of uprooting us and planting us somewhere more fertile. This card can be a reminder to reflect on whether you have given certain ideas, projects or relationships more importance than they are actually worth. As a result, this can lead to painful (but powerful) realizations. Allow yourself these new perspectives so that you can overcome the challenges and put yourself in more suitable and sustainable environments.

An unexpected change can make you feel as if everything you have been working for has been compromised. However, some endings can result in a release of pressure for you and ultimately bring you back into balance.

IMAGERY

See how a lightning bolt strikes the top of a tower and bursts into flames. This is a sign of the unexpected and how it can cause chaos and uncertainty. The lightning bolt may represent a sudden revelation or insight that ultimately brings your whole world crashing down around you.

The tower is perched on a rocky and inhospitable foundation, suggesting that you may have planted yourself or your dreams in an unsustainable or unrealistic environment.

The top of the tower being knocked off represents a connection to your crown chakra, which is how you receive divine insight/intelligence.

People leap from the windows – a sign that you should not care what awaits you, but should be more focused on accepting the fact that you cannot stay where you are.

The 12 small flames on the left represent the 12 signs of the Western zodiac and the 10 small flames on the right represent the 10 points on the tree of life. These are all reminders that, sometimes, unexpected change can be down to divine intervention. It may not make complete sense right now, but rest assured that, one day, things will become clear in hindsight.

17
The Star

KEY WORDS
Self-care · Inner reflection · Finding balance · Nurturing
Focused intention · Renewal · Spirituality

CARD MEANING

The Star card appears in a reading as a reminder that it is important to take time out once in a while. You need to prioritize self-care in order to find the energy that will help you to keep pushing forwards.

You also need to identify (and commit to) what is most important to you so that you can have an action plan moving forwards. This will help to combat any feelings of ambiguity that you may be struggling with. This card signifies the sheer amount of potential that can come from this self-reflection and redirection.

Sometimes this card represents receiving unexpected guidance from someone else. This can come in the form of the people around you, a spirit guide or sensing a lost loved one around you. Keep an eye out for signs such as feathers, butterflies and repeating numbers. This card in and of itself is a sign that all is well and that you are always in the right place at the right time. Commit to resting and healing and

when you are ready, you can work towards the things you have identified as being the most important to you. Your commitment will pay off in unexpected ways and this card is a reminder to stay focused.

IMAGERY

The woman pictured here is completely naked – a sign of vulnerability and exposure. She gazes at her reflection in a pool of water, symbolizing self-reflection and contemplation.

The woman has one foot on the ground and the other in the water, symbolic of the need for you to be practical and use your common sense while also honouring your emotions and intuition.

She holds a jug of water in each hand. One represents the subconscious and the other represents the conscious. Allow yourself to explore the things that might be influencing you in both of these areas.

She pours water into the pool and onto the ground next to her. This is a reminder that you need to nourish your environment/self with time, care and attention.

Small sprouts emerge from the ground around her, suggesting that new ideas can take root and grow, especially if you tend to them.

The big star above her head shows that, in order to find the direction you crave, you need to have a specific goal to focus on or work towards.

The five rivulets coming from the jug of water on the right represent the five senses and the importance of regulating your nervous system. You can fall out of balance when stressed, and prioritizing a period of rest can bring you back to a place of stability.

18
The Moon

KEY WORDS
Illusion · Uncertainty · Patience
Intuition · Release

CARD MEANING

In a reading, The Moon card serves as a reminder that there are always going to be times of uncertainty due to a lack of information. This card highlights the importance of being patient and the need to seek out more information in order to make better-informed decisions.

Like The High Priestess (see page 48), this card represents a time in life when what is right in front of you may not be accurately portraying the whole picture. Even though this card serves as a reminder for you to connect with your own intuition, it can represent the temptation to follow what is convenient rather than what is actually needed. Remember, convenience benefits the ego and intuition challenges it.

You may feel resistance to some of the changes that need to take place due to unprocessed thoughts/emotions, so reflect on these and ask yourself if any past experiences are shaping your current view. This is a card of patience and connection to the subconscious. It normally appears in a reading when

something is triggering a past fear and you feel a sense of urgency in finding a solution. Projecting past fears onto current experiences is only going to cause you to repeat old cycles over and over again. View this as an opportunity to reflect, meditate and change your approach to something. This card symbolizes a journey through your shadows and the profound truths that can be found from facing these head on instead of allowing them to subconsciously influence you. Be sure to set aside some time to contemplate on, and release, that which is no longer serving you.

IMAGERY

A path winds its way between two towers beneath a star-filled sky with a crescent moon. On one side of the path is a dog and on the other a wolf. Between them a crayfish crawls out of a pond.

The path leads off into the distance, symbolizing an opportunity to follow a higher path of consciousness.

The crescent-shaped moon is signifying that your intuition is only partly guiding you and that you need to sit and meditate to connect with this further.

The dog and the wolf represent the inner battle we sometimes feel between the conscious (tamed) and unconscious (untamed) aspects of ourselves. You might be fighting with different urges and unsure of which ones to listen to/follow.

The two towers standing tall in the distance are symbolic of your conflicting belief systems and the habits/routines you have picked up or accumulated in life.

The crayfish crawling out of the water represents a new idea or insight that arises into your consciousness and how patient meditation can allow you to access that information. You are most likely being shown a new path/perspective here and you should follow it, even if it seems unfamiliar.

19
The Sun

KEY WORDS

Joy · Acceptance · Empowerment
Authenticity · Stability

CARD MEANING

The Sun card appears as a reminder that you are safe to live your life in alignment with your true self (and desires) and to explore creative ventures that are in alignment with this. You have nothing to be ashamed of, or embarrassed about, and you are safe to put your whole self forward here by living in authenticity.

This card represents the power of positive energy and the impact this can have on yourself, your environment and your experiences. You can be a force for good by radiating this joy outwards. Being your true self will give so much more value to those around you. When you put your whole self forward, you are more likely to connect with others who share similar qualities or values, and this will allow them to express themselves more authentically too. If you choose to pretend to be someone other than who you are (for example, by acting nonchalantly about the things you care about), you will find yourself surrounded by those who do not share your same vision or path and you will ultimately sabotage yourself.

This card reminds you that you are allowed to feel optimistic about life. You should celebrate your wins and positive qualities and allow yourself to bask in joy and self-appreciation. This card shows that it is important to be connected to yourself, to your environment and to your deeper purpose.

This card can also be a great sign for pregnancy, childbearing, vitality and health.

IMAGERY

A child sits completely naked and exposed on top of a horse. This imagery is a sign of reconnecting with your own playful innocence and a reminder not to take everything too seriously all of the time.

The child's nudity is a sign that you have nothing to hide and should be accepting of your true form.

There are four sunflowers. The number four represents stability and balance, while the sunflowers stand for sustenance and joy. The more self-assured you become, the more stability you can create for yourself. You will be able to flourish (like a sunflower) by allowing yourself to be true to yourself and to the things that truly interest you.

The red feather coming from the child's head and the orange fabric billowing in the wind are both symbols of kundalini energy. The colours red and orange represent the lower two chakras (energy centres in our body), the root and sacral chakra. The root chakra represents your ability to trust the earth to support you and relates to survival and safety. The sacral chakra represents your expression of creativity and sexuality. Notice how the card is yellow – this represents the third chakra, the solar plexus chakra, which is the chakra of personal empowerment. Therefore, this card is a reminder that you will be able to move onwards and upwards if you embody these elements of self-expression.

The white colour of the horse symbolizes purity – the same purity that a child has before it becomes tainted by the world around it. It serves as a reminder to connect with your purest essence and allow yourself the opportunity to express yourself freely like a child would, with no apologies.

See how the sun radiates its vitality in all directions. This is symbolic of the way in which optimism, positivity and true expression can have a positive impact on your environment.

20
Judgment

KEY WORDS
Forgiveness · Healing · Acknowledgment
Acceptance · New purpose

CARD MEANING

When the Judgment card appears in a reading, it is asking you to come to terms with actions or events from the past (whether your own or those of someone else) and to be willing to acknowledge and accept them as a means to move forward. If you are ready to level up in your life, now is the time to embrace this higher level of consciousness by practising acceptance.

This card often appears when somebody is contemplating forgiveness and it highlights the importance of considering each point of view and remembering that there are many different complex forces at play that can take any one of us off track. You are ready to judge someone fairly or to be judged in return and this card is a reminder to use the wisdom gained from those experiences as a way to have a higher purpose moving forward.

This card sometimes represents an opportunity to connect with likeminded individuals who understand your journey

and want to share the experience with you – for example, members of an addiction recovery group, an emotional support group, a religious group. If you are wondering whether you will be able to move past a situation or not, this card is a great sign that you will – as long as you are ready to acknowledge and accept the past for what it is.

IMAGERY

A group of naked people rise up from their graves and await judgment from a spirit guide above. The image represents the importance of getting everything out in the open and trusting that you will be judged fairly.

The spirit guide is a symbol of your spiritual pursuits being called into question. Have you been acting in alignment with your morals? Are you holding onto grudges or are you willing to be forgiving and compassionate? Do not allow bitter or shameful feelings to distract you from your spiritual development.

The people have their arms outspread toward the spirit guide. This shows a willingness to move on from something and a desire to reconnect with someone (or even yourself).

The insurmountable mountains in the background remind you that some situations cannot be avoided or escaped. They must be faced head on.

21
The World

KEY WORDS
Completion · Paradigm shift · Wholeness · Ease
Success · Reflection

CARD MEANING

When The World card appears in a reading, it is a reminder that you have achieved a goal, desire or completed a cycle and should feel accomplished. This card can also represent promotions, graduations, marriages, pregnancies or any mid- to long-term goal that has come to fruition.

The card is a reminder that you are in the right place at the right time and should be proud of your progress. Do not forget just how far you have come to get to this point, as a little reflection can go a very long way. As much as this card symbolizes success, looking back at your past experiences and challenges and identifying the wisdom and value that has been gained from them should be acknowledged and taken forward with you.

If there are still any loose ends, this is a sign to deal with them so that you can move forward and leave the past in the past. This card can also be a sign of worldwide travel, for leisure, adventure, studies or work. You could find an appreciation for a new culture as a part of the next step of your journey.

IMAGERY

A woman looks back towards the past with her head but towards the future with her body. This is symbolic of one cycle closing and another beginning. The woman's head is reflecting on the journey she has been on, while her body is ready to jump into the next cycle.

The giant wreath surrounding the woman is a symbol of the continuous cycles we go through in life and how one thing cannot begin without another thing ending. It also represents the portal she is jumping through to begin her next cycle. (You are levelling up and going through a paradigm shift!)

The batons in her hands are like the batons on The Magician card (see page 44) and show that a desire/goal has finally manifested or is very close to being reached.

In each corner of the card is a fixed sign of the Western zodiac: Aquarius, Taurus, Leo, Scorpio. The four also represent the four seasons and the four elements. Remember, fours stand for stability; although we go through cycles of change, these are ultimately reliable and stable.

THE
MINOR
ARCANA

This section looks at the four suits of the **Minor Arcana**:

Wands represent our passion, desires and creativity.

Swords represent our ideas, belief systems and mental processing.

Cups represent our emotions, feelings, intuition and relationships.

Coins represent career, finances, stability and the material realm.

Ace of Wands

KEY WORDS
Fresh starts
New beginnings
New ideas
Creativity
Seize the moment

CARD MEANING

When the Ace of Wands appears in a reading, it represents a new idea in an area that you are passionate or excited about. This card is the perfect reminder for you to take bold steps forward and to seize any opportunities that arise before they fizzle out and pass you by. It is asking you to run away with your new ideas and follow your heart. Allow yourself to envision something exciting for yourself. There is a reason that you feel drawn towards certain things and you should feel encouraged to explore any exciting new ideas. If you are contemplating whether or not to pursue a new project, this card is a huge YES. It is a sign that you need to follow your intuition and listen to your gut instincts. This card represents the spark needed to create something exciting, however you must tend to the flames if you want whatever you create to be long-lasting.

IMAGERY

A hand reaches out from a cloud and grabs a sprouting wand. This represents a new opportunity or idea that you need to grab with both hands, and that has the potential to grow into something more if you tend to it!

The fertile landscape in the background represents the potential for something to flourish if you give it the right environment in which to grow.

The hills and mountains are symbolic of the challenges you may face further down the line but that can easily be overcome. Try not to concern yourself too much with future concerns. It is great to be prepared, however it is also important that you do not talk yourself out of things before they have even begun!

There is a castle on a hill in the background. This is a sign of the success that can be found by exploring a new idea and taking it to its limits.

Remember that when you hold a wand and make a wish you have a clear intention in mind. This card is a reminder that focused intention can result in magic if you believe in yourself and commit to it.

Two of Wands

KEY WORDS
Decisions
Choices
Planning
Action
Optimism

CARD MEANING

The appearance of the Two of Wands in a reading is often a sign that you are feeling inspired, but are still in the planning stages of a new endeavour.

The card is a wonderful sign of the abundance that could be available to you if you are willing to step outside of your comfort zone.

Wands represent passion, desire and creativity, so you should embrace new ideas and opportunities that are sparked in this area. The card is a clear sign that you know what you want to accomplish (the Ace of Wands) and that now is the time to come up with an action plan. The card can also represent the thought of overseas travel, further studies or a career change that will expand your horizons. It is urging you to follow this spark and take your chances.

IMAGERY

The man pictured quite literally has the world in his hands. It is a clear sign that you are aware of the abundance that is available to you, but are still considering your options. The man stands within the confines of his home, once again showing that you have not yet ventured outside of your comfort zone and are still in the planning phase of something.

The two wands on either side of the man represent the different options that are available to you. One is fixed to the wall (staying where you are) and the other is free from the wall (venturing past your comfort zone).

The man is grasping the second wand, which is symbolic of the urge to pursue the bolder option. You are being encouraged to make the bold decision here.

The verdant nature in the background hints at the abundance that is available to you should you decide to leave your comfort zone.

The mountains signify that this new journey will not come without its challenges, but that you do not need to concern yourself with those just yet.

Three of Wands

---◆---

KEY WORDS
Focus
Commitment
Foresight
Combining elements
Dedication
Success

---✕---

CARD MEANING

The Three of Wands is a reminder that you need to commit yourself over a long period of time in order to reach your goals. It also urges you to think bigger for yourself and not to be afraid to broaden your horizons even further. The fact that you can see far ahead in this picture shows that you are more than prepared for any challenges that lie ahead. Be assured that you have the ability to prepare for what lies ahead and there is nothing to worry about in the immediate future.

This is a fantastic card for career development as it represents commitment and success in your endeavours. It is also a reminder for you to use your common sense to guide you. However, it is worth noting that this can hold you back if you neglect to fan the inner spark of creativity that started this venture in the first place. At times you must invest your time and energy, but you must also find time to recharge so that you do not burn out. This card reminds you of the importance of balance when it comes to being successful. It also represents travel, so is a reminder to be adventurous and open to any opportunities that broaden your horizons.

IMAGERY

A man gazes off into the far distance from a cliff top and is symbolic of the need for you to see the bigger picture and to prepare yourself for upcoming challenges.

The three wands are firmly planted in the ground, signifying that, it is possible to commit to your current goals while also envisioning something greater for yourself.

The man has left the comfort of his home, suggesting that you have willingly ventured into new territory. Be proud of your courage, bravery and dedication to your own development.

The wreath on the man's head is a sign of the success you have already achieved and carry forward with you.

The three sailing ships symbolize slow and steady progress and signify potential movement or expansion overseas.

The broad horizon is a sign that, although you have left your comfort zone, you still need to think about the bigger picture.

Four of Wands

KEY WORDS
Celebration
Milestone
Achievement
Satisfaction
Rite of passage

CARD MEANING

The Four of Wands is a reminder of just how important it is to celebrate your achievements in life with your friends, family members and loved ones – whether an engagement party, wedding, business expansion, birthday, homecoming, promotion or just a regular old party to let your hair down.

The card is asking you to pause and see how far you have come, and to remember all the hard work and commitment it took to get there. This is the time to enjoy the fruit of your labour. Of course, more work lies ahead, but for now you can celebrate what you have accomplished already and enjoy the company of others. You deserve to have a little break.

This card represents security so you can trust that you are safe here. You should feel very satisfied with your progress.

IMAGERY

Two people throw their hands up together in celebration. This clearly represents a moment of victory!

The many flowers in this scene signify abundance, growth and success.

There is much merriment in the background – a sign that you have the support of friends or family members, and that they want to share and celebrate your accomplishments.

The four upright wands are in the 11:11 position – a number associated with wish fulfilment! Be sure to celebrate the small (or big) wins and enjoy letting your hair down.

Five of Wands

KEY WORDS
Competition
Diversity
Chaotic energy
Overcoming obstacles
Standing strong

CARD MEANING

The Five of Wands appears in a reading to remind you that, although working in a team environment can be incredibly expansive and efficient, sometimes it can also cause division and instability. As the famous saying goes: 'Too many cooks spoil the broth.' When this card appears, it signifies that you (or someone else) may need to listen to others and let go of the idea that your way is best. There is a big difference between confidence and arrogance. Ask yourself: 'Is it more productive to stand up and vocalize something I believe will help the situation or would it be wiser to remove myself from the chaos and observe/listen instead?'. Whatever your normal approach is, be willing to try the opposite. Remain open to new perspectives or insight. It is worth remembering that we need people to challenge us so that we can grow, but we also need to keep an eye on how productive we are. Fives represent change and you have something to gain from those who are different to you. This card is ultimately an opportunity for you to take control of an unclear situation and implement a clear plan moving forwards.

IMAGERY

See how these five people fight for control of an unstable situation. This card is symbolic of the chaos and confusion that can happen when working in a team environment. (This can include families and friendships too.)

Each person has different clothing, representing diversity, but also a lack of true understanding of one another. This can suggest an opportunity to learn from each other and to listen to each person's unique perspective/approach.

The wands (ideas) overlap each other. This signifies that there are always multiple approaches and it would be wise to listen and learn from each other.

The wands collide, but no one is struck. This suggests that you should try not to take anything personally: remember that it is the group vs the problem and not the group vs you.

The desolate and dry ground is a reminder to check in with how productive (and therefore abundant) this environment is.

Six of Wands

KEY WORDS
Achievements
Shared goals
Recognition
Appreciation
Inspiration

CARD MEANING

The Six of Wands represents the importance of recognition and appreciation for motivation, whether it comes in the form of a positive review from/toward your boss or peers, an award for something you or someone else has been working on, or just a pat on the back from/for someone close to you. This card can sometimes be a sign of public recognition that results in a major confidence boost.

The card is all about overcoming the chaos of the Five of Wands and working with others on a shared mission or goal. So, remember to stay focused and appreciative of those who are sharing this journey with you. You are being reminded to believe in yourself and others and be proud of your efforts. We all deserve recognition, and we deserve to be able to celebrate and flaunt it sometimes too. You are being asked to put yourself out there and be proud of what you are working on. Keep in mind, as it's a number six, you are not quite at the finish line yet so keep pushing forwards and use this milestone as a means for extra motivation.

IMAGERY

The figure on the card rides through a crowd of cheering people with a victory wreath on her head. This is a very clear sign of success. You have made it through the chaos of the Five of Wands.

A crowd cheers the figure on, signifying recognition, appreciation and achievement and is symbolic of the importance of sharing mutual goals and interests with the people around you.

The white horse is a symbol of both progress (or travel) and purity. It is a sign that your intentions are in the right place and that you deserve to be celebrated.

The figure holds her wand raised up in the air and it is also adorned with a victory wreath. This suggests that you should be proud to show off your accomplishments and allow yourself or someone else the recognition you/they deserve.

Seven of Wands

KEY WORDS
Conviction
Defence
Determination
Triumph
Bravery

CARD MEANING

The Seven of Wands signifies a period in your life where you can (and should) prove yourself. The card represents being in an enviable position that others might be tempted to challenge/dismantle. It is worth remembering that you will very rarely receive negative criticism or condemnation from people who are doing better than you. This card hints at you being caught off guard and finding yourself scrambling to defend your position but feeling somewhat unprepared.

The Seven of Wands invites you to stand up for yourself, defend your ground and hold onto what you believe is right. The reason people envy you is normally because they want to be where you are and they may try to discredit you as a way to feel better about where they currently are. This can manifest in the form of our friends, family members, or colleagues, but is most hurtful from the people that we personally recognize. You may feel betrayed when this happens, but this card is an important reminder to remain on higher ground and not allow other people's belief systems to compromise your own.

This card can also represent times when you may be feeling overwhelmed by many different things at once. Multiple things might be fighting for your attention, however if you strategize a plan moving forwards, you can address everything one step at a time.

IMAGERY

The person on this card is clearly outnumbered by a gang of six wands. This represents a situation in which you may feel 'ganged up on' or where you are having to attack multiple problems at once.

The person wears two different shoes, symbolic of something catching you off guard and you worrying about whether you have a strong enough leg to stand on.

This person still has the higher ground – a reminder that anyone you are dealing with is looking up to you and most likely envious of where you are. Do not take their criticism to heart. They just want to be where you are.

Eight of Wands

KEY WORDS
Rapid movement
Momentum
Resolution
Mobility after stagnation
Impending conclusion

CARD MEANING

When the Eight of Wands appears in a reading, you are being asked to have a clear path moving forward. Following the Seven of Wands, you now have the space and freedom to progress with your plans as you have been able to overcome any challenges of self-doubt and criticism. Now you can be laser focused on your goals without distraction. If you are waiting to hear important news, this card is a sign of getting a clear-cut answer or a resolution soon.

When things start to progress with speed, it is important that you go with the flow instead of trying to fight against it. Once certain plans are in motion, there is no stopping them. As you near the closing of a deal or oath, you need to make sure that you are not cutting any corners.

You are being asked to dive into this experience headfirst and to be as productive as possible. You should not wait around when this card makes an appearance but must take action as soon as you can. Strike while the iron is hot, as they say! As this is a card of action, it can also symbolize movement or travel. You may even benefit from a last-minute getaway to recharge yourself.

IMAGERY

Eight sprouted wands fly through the air with great speed. This represents focus, precision and progress being made. Think of an arrow flying through the air to reach its target – you are in motion and there is no stopping you now.

The bright sky signifies a clear mind after recovering from the challenges of the Seven of Wands.

The serene green valley in the distance is symbolic of the abundance and growth that will be gained from this focus and hard work.

Nine of Wands

KEY WORDS
Extreme exertion
Reflection
Replenishment
Commitment
Perseverance

CARD MEANING

The Nine of Wands appears in a reading when you are feeling run-down or doubtful that you can actually cross the finish line. Although you might be feeling exhausted from the long journey you have embarked on, this card is a reminder to keep pushing forward. You are so close to the finish line now and all your hard work will be rewarded, but only if you do not give up.

Remember to reflect on everything that you have gone through to get to this point. You have overcome so many challenges and you are more than capable of pushing past this final hurdle. Do not forget to replenish your energy so that you can remain focused moving forward. Your attention needs to stay keen if you want to keep things up to standard.

This card is a sign that you are more than able to hit the target and persevere against all odds. You are being asked to put everything you have into this final leg of the journey so that you can relax later by knowing that you put your best self forward.

IMAGERY

An injured man stands clutching his wand with eight past wands looming over him. The scene is a symbol of the challenges you have overcome and the toll they have taken on you. You may be feeling overwhelmed about everything you have yet to accomplish but remember that nines represent nearing completion, and this is the final hurdle before you can cross that finish line!

The blue sky beyond the wands is a sign that freedom is nearby.

The bandaged wounds symbolize the toll this journey has taken on you.

The nine wands symbolize the wisdom and experiences you have accumulated along the way.

Ten of Wands

KEY WORDS
Success
Responsibilities
Delegation
Boundaries
Exhaustion
Burnout

CARD MEANING

The Ten of Wands is a reminder that success comes with a burden of responsibilities and sometimes these can catch up with you. Perhaps you are juggling too many things at once or you are trying to get everything done by yourself. If you want to be sustainable, you are going to have to delegate to others, accept help and be willing to say no to extra demands.

This card suggests that you can experience burnout from taking on too much at once. Remember, the number ten is a sign that you have made so much progress to get to a point where you once dreamed you could be. It is also a reminder that the exhaustion you are feeling is only temporary.

Keep pushing forward and try to assess which tasks are most important so you can prioritize your energy accordingly. Start saying no to extra demands and try delegating tasks out to others. If you ignore this advice and try to do everything at once, you will experience a burnout.

Learn to lighten the load so you can be more productive and cross that finish line more efficiently. Do not let the illusion of holding everything together fool you. Make sure you are not prioritizing maintenance over growth, otherwise you may lose touch with the spark that started all of this in the first place.

IMAGERY

This person is struggling to carry the weight of ten wands. It is a sign that you have a lot of responsibility on your shoulders right now and you are probably trying to achieve too much by yourself.

The person's back is bending under the weight, symbolic of feeling weighed down and physically exhausted and close to burnout/collapse.

The person's house is close by in the background, signifying that you are very near to the finish line and that you will soon be able to put that heavy load down. Soon you will be able to share your insight/experiences with the people waiting to meet you.

Page of Wands

KEY WORDS
Studious
Enthusiasm
Openness to learning
Fresh ideas
Optimism
Self-consciousness
Encouragement

CARD MEANING

The Page of Wands appears in a reading when you are feeling inspired and curious about a new idea, somewhat similar to the Ace of Wands. Whereas the Ace of Wands represents seizing the moment, the Page of Wands encourages you to embrace more of a studious energy. It is inviting you to try anything you currently feel pulled towards and to be willing to have an openness to learning.

The card suggests you should embrace each opportunity and see where it takes you. Although the card has a very playful and youthful energy, you would be wise to listen to those with more experience than you. Your openness to learning will work in your favour here. Be willing to accept that you do not have all the knowledge needed just yet and you may have to go searching for it. You may even find yourself feeling self-conscious at times due to a lack of experience, however you are being asked to venture past your comfort zone so that you can explore your own potential. Give yourself time to adjust to these changes and remember to show yourself compassion as you embrace the learning process.

This card has a very positive energy when representing somebody else. You can trust that they are putting their best foot forward and even if they can be self-conscious, they are willing to try their best at all times.

IMAGERY

The Page gazes in curiosity at the leaves sprouting from his wand. This represents an inquisitiveness about his own growth/potential.

The wand is planted firmly in the ground, signifying that, although he is inspired by something, the Page does not know how to take action on it just yet.

The salamanders on his tunic are associated with fire and magic and therefore creativity.

The barren land is a sign that you can find inspiration and growth in the most unlikely places.

The mountains symbolize challenges yet to be overcome.

Knight of Wands

KEY WORDS
Action
Impulsivity
Charisma
Loyalty
Self-discovery
Adventure
Movement

CARD MEANING

The Knight of Wands appears as encouragement for you to take action on the things that truly move/inspire you. This is a sign that you are ready to face an issue head on and that you are prepared to take things to the next level. You may feel an urge to explore the world around you and this card can sometimes represent movement, travel or a change in residence.

This card serves as a reminder that you are not always aware of the raw power that lies within you, and sometimes you will feel the need to search outside of yourself to get a deeper understanding of who you are. Your willingness to venture outside of your comfort zone and to commit to exploring yourself will allow you to figure out what you want and what you are truly capable of.

The card normally represents somebody with loyal, charismatic, fair and protective qualities, so if it is representing somebody else, you can definitely trust them. Such a person can sometimes come across as overbearing and this is because they are very passionate but deep down they are in need of some kindness. Trust in them and they will help you to move things into action.

IMAGERY

The Knight holds up a sprouting wand, symbolic of a willingness to take action and dive into things head on!

His horse is rearing before charging forward as a sign of readiness and anticipation

The salamanders on his robe are associated with fire and creativity.

Flames trail behind the Knight's body and head, signifying intense passion and vehemence. Think trailblazer!

The barren landscape serves as a reminder that it's not your environment that defines you but what you can create from it.

Queen of Wands

KEY WORDS
Leadership
Generosity
Warmth
Charisma
Authenticity
Feistiness
Gracefulness

CARD MEANING

The Queen of Wands represents the divine feminine embodiment of Wand/Fire energy. This card represents somebody who has great leadership potential and naturally commands the attention of others. Remember, this card could be representing you or somebody else that you can learn from. Regardless of this, it is asking you to be bold in your actions. Do not be afraid to step into your power and broadcast yourself honestly in the world.

The Queen of Wands influences the people around them for the better. They are generous, open and giving, but may come across as intimidating at first. It can represent someone that leaves a lasting impress on on you or is symbolic of the lasting impression you can leave with others (whether you truly believe this or not). The Queen of Wands is feisty and naturally commanding. If this is representing somebody else, ask yourself if you are truly intimidated by them or if there is something about them that you aspire to be.

This card is a reminder that we all have a shadow side, whether this is a dark sense of humour or some kind of past trauma or loss. Do not be afraid to take ownership of your darker side. This darkness will allow you to connect with others on a much deeper level and therefore have a more significant impact. You may be able to relate to this person more than you realize, or others with you

IMAGERY

The Queen sits on a throne decorated with lions, an animal that represents strength, ferocity and power.

The sunflowers surrounding the Queen symbolize joy, growth and contentment.

The colour yellow is often associated with the solar plexus chakra (the third energy centre in the body), which represents personal empowerment, authenticity and expression.

A black cat sits at the Queen's feet. This is a sign that you should be in touch with your darker/shadow self. You should not be embarrassed by this, however you may not make this immediately apparent to others.

King of Wands

KEY WORDS
Authority
Maturity
Power
Charisma
Confidence
Generous leader

CARD MEANING

The King of Wands represents the divine masculine embodiment of Wand/Fire energy. The card represents a confident leader, who not only believes in himself and his own ideas but actually encourages and enlists other people to help him achieve them (and their own) as well.

This card can represent either an opportunity for you to step into a more leadership focused role and guide people towards a shared objective, or to learn from someone who is already in this position. It suggests that we can sometimes get the 'impossible' done when we both believe in it and enjoy the process. With much more maturity and experience than the

Knight of Wands, the King of Wands is actually able to see his goals through to the end and lead others to do the same. He is less impulsive and more productive.

This card can represent a fantastic business partner, romantic partner or friend who will help you move things into action. The card can also be a reminder to slow down and enjoy the process and to focus on the smaller details. Achieving the goal is not necessarily the main objective here, it has more to do with being a part of something greater than yourself and remembering to enjoy the ride. Make sure you are bringing your visions to life by giving them your full time and attention.

IMAGERY

The King sits confidently on his throne, clearly showing his authority and ability to influence others.

The sprouting wand in his hand is a symbol of creativity.

The salamanders on his cape are eating their own tails and symbolize passion and creativity.

The small salamander at the bottom-right-hand corner signifies that you can find joy and inspiration from the small things in life.

Ace of Swords

KEY WORDS
Mental clarity
Fresh insight
Determination
Reflection
New approach
Important information

CARD MEANING

When the Ace of Swords appears in a reading, it represents a new approach or a new way of thinking that is going to be beneficial for your development. It is asking you to be open to new information or to be willing to go in search of it. The card symbolizes a new solution to something about which you have been waiting for an answer. It is a sign that an opportunity for clarity is nearby and that you will know exactly what you have to do to progress.

A sword can be double edged, so consider carefully how you can use this new information for the benefit of all, and not just for selfish reasons. As Aces represent new beginnings, this card can symbolize an opportunity for you to learn something new or to take on a more 'visionary' role. Embrace new information that comes your way and implement it moving forwards. Pay close attention to your words and thoughts. These will shape your reality and are far more powerful than you think.

IMAGERY

A hand clutches an upright sword and represents the need to grasp new information (or a new insight).

The hand emerges from a cloud, a symbol of this information coming from divine intervention/intelligence.

The crown and wreath draped across the top of the sword symbolize the value that can be gained from taking an intellectual approach.

The jagged mountains in the distance are a sign of the worry and stress that can arise from the rocky times that lie ahead.

Two of Swords

KEY WORDS
Denial
Avoidance
Repression
Failure to make a decision
Struggle

CARD MEANING

The Two of Swords symbolizes a time in life where you feel torn between your heart and your mind, and do not know which one to listen to. This inner conflict can tempt you into putting off a decision. However, it is worth bearing in mind that this is not a position anyone can hold indefinitely. You may like to weigh up the pros and cons of each approach so that you can make informed and well-balanced decisions but delaying things too much can also lead to overwhelm.

This card signifies that you may be lacking information or you have had the wool pulled over your eyes. Reflect on whether this is a blindfold you have put there yourself to avoid making a decision or addressing an issue, or whether someone else has led you astray. Make sure that you are doing your best to be fully informed and try to commit yourself to a clear decision moving forwards. Otherwise you may exhaust yourself trying to maintain things as they are. Change, although painful, is necessary for growth.

IMAGERY

The card shows a blindfolded woman, symbolizing that you are not seeing everything clearly. You may not see a straight solution to a current problem, or you may not have all of the information needed to make a decision. You may also have had the 'wool pulled over your eyes', either by yourself or by somebody else. The woman holds two swords in perfect balance with one another, showing that you are weighing up your thoughts and emotions and carefully considering each side of a situation.

There is a body of water behind the woman. Although swords represent intellect, the water imagery suggests that emotional aspects are an important or influencing part of this decision-making process.

The islands in the water signify the challenges that come with making the decision. There is no clear-cut pathway here and things must be navigated carefully.

The small crescent moon in the top right corner is a sign that you are going to have to use your intuition to help navigate the situation.

Three of Swords

KEY WORDS
Personal growth
Disappointment
Betrayal
Painful truth
Loss

CARD MEANING

The Three of Swords symbolizes hurt and disappointment, the three different swords suggesting that you have probably been hurt in more ways than one. This card can represent the unexpected betrayals or losses that arise and catch us off guard. It definitely has a 'door slammed in the face' energy about it, when it feels as if your way forward has been compromised. There is no denying how hurtful loss and disappointment can be, but this is also an opportunity for you to have an emotional release. You may find that you need to open the floodgates and have a good old cry to let those feelings of sadness and disappointment flow through you.

This card also serves as a reminder to focus on the recovery process rather than hyper-fixating on what you have lost.

While the pain may cloud your experience for a while, this stormy time will pass just as the clouds in the sky do. It may take weeks or months but remember to be patient with yourself and the process. Do not take on anyone's hurtful words as the 'truth' and do not forget to look at what learning can be gained from the situation. This is a card of profound growth that can only come from disappointment. You will need to give yourself time to heal from this loss.

IMAGERY

A heart is pierced through by three swords, clearly depicting something that has caused a significant amount of emotional turmoil or pain.

The three swords can represent hurtful words, actions and intentions.

The card has a stormy environment – a sign of emotional disturbance, yet also a reminder that just like clouds in the sky, this too shall pass.

Four of Swords

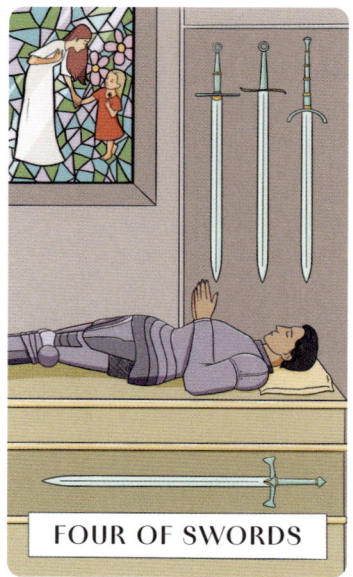

KEY WORDS
Respite from difficulty
Meditation
Reflection
Gratitude
Recuperation

CARD MEANING

When the Four of Swords appears in a reading, it serves as a reminder of the benefits that can come from taking a breather and refocusing yourself before making important decisions. This card is a symbol of getting over difficult or stressful times, such as going through a separation, experiencing the loss of a loved one, losing your way or any other painful or confusing experiences that can cause you to worry about the future and what that might look like for you.

It represents a period of time following the Three of Swords during which you reflect on your losses and eventually find the wisdom that can be gained from them. It is worth bearing in mind that this wisdom cannot be found without a little reflection. This is also probably not the time to be making any major life decisions as you may still be mentally clouded from these recent experiences.

Whether you feel you need this rest or not does not matter, you have to prioritize taking time out every now and again to recharge. This card represents a busy mind, and so taking time out can be very beneficial in helping you become more focused and productive in general.

The Four of Swords is often referred to as the meditation card. Reconnecting with the present moment and your breath will prevent you fantasizing about what you wish had happened instead or worrying about everything that could go wrong moving forward. Reconnecting with your breath will allow you to be more centred when making important life decisions.

IMAGERY

A person holds their hands together in contemplation or prayer, signifying that something is taking up a lot of their mental space and that they might be praying for a resolution to something. Three swords point down towards the person and a fourth sword lies beneath them.

The three swords pointing down towards the person symbolize that you feel very on edge and are frightened of being hurt.

The person is fully armoured, signifying that you are in self-protect mode and need to prioritize your mental wellbeing and safety.

The single sword laying beneath the person is a sign that you need to have a singular focus/approach moving forwards.

In the top-left-hand corner is a stained-glass window depicting a woman and child. This shows that you are in need of guidance and is a reminder that you are deserving of compassion and consolation.

Five of Swords

KEY WORDS
Personal gain
Dishonour
Spitefulness
Humiliation
Bullying

CARD MEANING

The Five of Swords is a reminder to navigate conflict maturely and without self-interest. Try your best to let go of the need to be right or the need to prove a point. Hammering in your own point of view can result in you losing the trust of the people around you and you may find your relationships suffering because of this. You have to ask yourself if it is really worth it.

This card is a sign that you need to pick your battles wisely, and that you must not lose yourself by trying to prove a point. Be willing to acknowledge where you might have gone wrong in this area and try to make amends as a way to move forwards.

If you are currently feeling satisfied in proving a point to somebody, this card is a sign that your satisfaction will be short-lived, and you need to reflect on the losses that come paired with this, such as compromising your values or the trust within your relationships. Let go of the need to prove yourself and make sure you are not compromising any of your values moving forwards.

If you were on the receiving end of this encounter, the card is asking you not to brood in the disappointment for too long. If you do, you may find yourself becoming disillusioned and feeling more pessimistic about the future. Accept your losses and try to learn from this experience instead. It may be wise to cut this person off and not engage in any further conflict with them, especially if they are not taking the time to consider your point of view or your emotional wellbeing. Nobody wins in this kind of scenario, and it is best to remove yourself from it as soon as possible.

IMAGERY

The person in the foreground is grasping three swords and almost smirking as if they are proud of what they have accomplished. This is a sign that somebody is gaining some kind of pleasure or satisfaction from being selfish and putting their own needs or point of view first.

Two individuals walk away from this person. You can clearly see the emotional distance the conflict has caused between everyone. The most distant person is slouched over in disappointment and defeat.

Two swords lie on the ground – a sign of that which has been lost or compromised.

The sky is very stormy, windy and tumultuous, a sign of a very chaotic or intense environment.

There is water in the distance, a symbol of the emotional impacts of this conflict.

Six of Swords

KEY WORDS
Overcoming adversity
Transition
Fresh start
Travel
Movement
Assistance

CARD MEANING

The Six of Swords is normally a sign that you are going through a transitionary period where things feel a bit disorienting. You may be between jobs, relationships or a little unsure about where you stand in general. Being uprooted from your past life might make it feel as if things are a bit up in the air but try and view this as a way to be replanted somewhere better.

This card represents feeling cautious of the unknown, however you do not need to be afraid. This card is also symbolic of a fresh start and the end of a difficult situation. Following the Five of Swords, it signifies a period of time during which you are finding respite and moving forward from your struggles.

You need to be willing to ask for help. Do not let stubborn self-reliance get in the way of receiving guidance from those around you. Try not to hyperfocus on the past but instead focus on what you would like to move towards.

If you are feeling weighed down by past experiences, this card is asking you to show yourself some grace and identify what you need to leave behind so that you can move forward with more ease. Whether this is a relationship, belief system, pattern of behaviour or past hurt, you can choose to put this down and have a new purpose moving forward.

IMAGERY

The card shows a boat moving from stormy and tumultuous waters into smooth and tranquil waters and is a sign that you are transitioning from an unstable environment into a calmer and safer one. A woman in the boat finds shelter and protection beneath a blanket and a young child nestles into her for comfort. This is a sign that you are still processing the experiences that led you to this point.

Six swords stand upright in the boat, signifying that you are still holding onto the lessons from this past experience.

A man paddles the boat forwards, representing the need to accept assistance and direction from others as a way to make progress.

The water and land imagery is symbolic of travel, relocation of some kind or maybe even movement overseas.

Seven of Swords

KEY WORDS
Sneakiness
Courage
Betrayal
Innovative risk
Potential loss or success

CARD MEANING

The Seven of Swords normally signifies sneaky or deceitful behaviour. When representing another person, the card should be perceived as a warning against their motivations and intentions.

However, context varies depending on the cards surrounding it. For example, it can represent removing yourself from a situation that is no longer beneficial for you or where you are not getting the recognition or treatment you deserve. This card can suggest the need to put your own interests first, even if it means disappointing somebody else. For example, letting your boss down so that you can prioritize your family instead.

On the other hand, the card can highlight dishonesty. When you lie, you are at risk of being found out. It can also be a sign of running away from your responsibilities or not facing something head on. As this card symbolizes sneaky behaviour, you may try to find shortcuts or try to bypass a traditional way of doing things. You may be in a situation where you try to think on your feet in order to win and this has the potential to succeed or fail. Definitely use the cards surrounding it to understand its meaning further.

IMAGERY

The person featured here is sneaking away from a situation with five swords in tow. This represents somebody putting their own needs first. The fact that the blades are dangerously close to this individual's shoulders should serve as a reminder that you are still at risk of being hurt or negatively affected by being selfish and you should handle this situation carefully.

The person is moving from a busy chaotic environment into a more peaceful one, a sign that maybe you need to take some respite from a certain environment.

The person's smile represents the feeling of satisfaction from getting away unnoticed. You may get away with a lie and feel proud of yourself for it. Remembering and being in touch with your motives is key to balance here. Do not lose sight of your morals/values.

Two swords get left behind, signifying that some things are inevitably lost as a part of the process.

Eight of Swords

KEY WORDS
Immobility
Self-doubt
Obliviousness
Feeling trapped
Victim mentality

CARD MEANING

The Eight of Swords appears in a reading when you are surrounded with so many mental concerns that it makes it feel almost impossible to find a way forwards. The card is a sign that you are not currently seeing the bigger picture and might even be unaware of your own obliviousness.

Perhaps you do not want to face a situation head on or accept it for how it truly is. However, in order to overcome this stagnant energy you will have to acknowledge that things will not go the way you want and focus on what you can control instead.

This card is a sign of your own self-limiting beliefs and how these are holding you hostage. Whether relevant to an unfulfilling job or relationship, you are stuck on the idea of something rather than facing the reality of it. You may be putting something off and this is only harming you further.

You may feel trapped right now, but you are capable of getting out of this place if you really want to. Gaining a new perspective is key. Take this card as a reminder that what you do not change, you choose – and you could choose a different reality for yourself if you really wanted to (and actually committed yourself to it).

You may be waiting to be rescued by somebody else, but this card represents the empowerment you can find from being decisive in your own actions as a way to move on from something or someone. You do have choices, even if you do not like your options.

This card often appears when you do not know if you should stay or go, however you should take this card as a sign that it is time to move on. You need to be willing to listen to your intuition, even if it makes you uncomfortable. You have the answer already and now is the time to take action.

IMAGERY

The card shows a woman who is bound and blindfolded and is symbolic of your not seeing a situation clearly. However, it is worth noting that if you took this blindfold (avoidance) off, you would realize that there is a way out of this.

The eight swords surrounding the woman represent the many mental concerns you may have and the feeling of being trapped.

There is water by the woman's feet – a sign that even though you might not be seeing the situation clearly, you are still in touch with your intuition and should listen to this, even if it makes you feel uncomfortable.

The home in the distance signifies that you are closer to comfort than you realize.

Nine of Swords

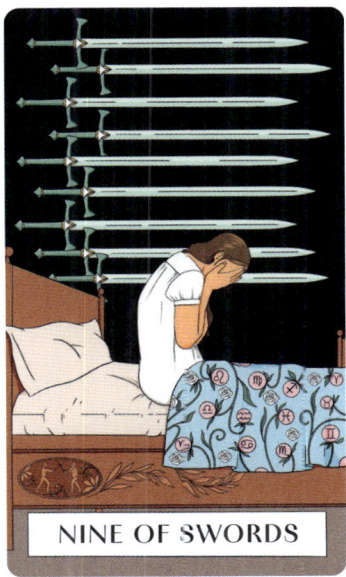

KEY WORDS
Mental anguish
Concern
Sleeplessness
Stress
Anxiety
Worry
Fear

CARD MEANING

When the Nine of Swords appears in a reading it is a sign that you need to check in with yourself to gauge how much energy you are expending on worrying and contemplating all of the worst-case scenarios. You may be feeling particularly stressed at the moment, or even suffering with insomnia, but your brain needs some rest if you want it to be able to work optimally. This card is a reminder to let go of things that are outside your control. For example, dwelling on what other people might think or feel or what could go wrong is not a productive use of your time and energy. You may have some dark and pessimistic thoughts but it is important to remember they are just thoughts. Until reality proves otherwise, you should treat them as such. This card represents a feeling of imminent threat and therefore you are probably feeling more anxious than usual and could benefit from regulating your nervous system with things such as mindfulness, breathwork or meditation.

The more you obsess over what is not working, the more evidence you are going to find around you to confirm your fears. This card is a sign that your current mental state may not be an accurate representation of what is actually happening and that you are overthinking. When this card appears you are being urged to reach out for help, specifically to somebody who can view the situation more logically. A third-party perspective will be very insightful and help you to see the light at the end of the tunnel. You do not have to go through this struggle alone.

IMAGERY

This person sits upright in bed with their head in their hands. It is very clear that there is some kind of sleeplessness or stress. You may be having nightmares or feel like you are living one. The nine swords hanging up on the wall next to them represent the heavy thoughts and stressors that are weighing on your mind.

An engraving on the side of the bed depicts two people engaged in battle. This represents a fear of conflict.

The blanket is patterned with roses and astrological signs, signifying that there is still hope and spiritual protection.

Ten of Swords

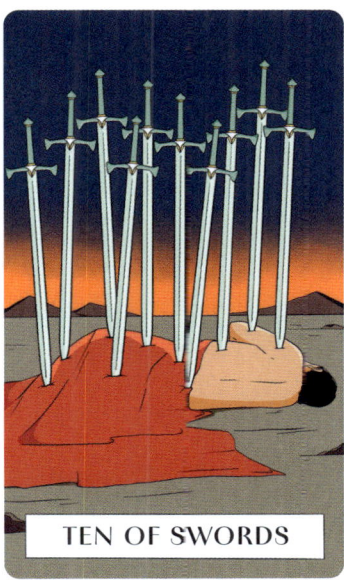

KEY WORDS
Outdated ways of being or thinking
Surrender
Liberation
Forgiveness

CARD MEANING

The Ten of Swords serves as a reminder to check in with the views in your mind that have grown past the point of being useful. Some of the habits (or relationships) that may have helped you (or felt good) in the past are not always going to be in alignment with the person that you want to become.

This card often represents something that you have struggled with over a significant period of time. Perhaps you have a habit that you just cannot seem to break out of or maybe someone close to you keeps on making false promises. This card highlights the repetitive cycles we engage in that keep us stuck and stagnant.

It is important that you reflect on the ways in which you might have done this in your own journey as well as taking a look at the people around you and ask yourself if they are really committed to change and growth. Some say that the definition of madness is to do the same thing over and over again and yet expect a different result and this card can represent a period in your life where you have reached a stalemate and have no other option than to choose a different pathway.

Remember, the number ten represents completion and therefore this suggests that you feel somewhat ready to leave this repetitive cycle behind you and create space for something new. Nobody else can force you to give this up, it is you who has to decide that you want to change. Be willing to create more space in your life for new relationships, behaviours, belief systems or habits.

This card can represent something that once symbolized a lot of potential to you so this can be a very painful process. Surrender to the situation for what it is and liberate yourself from the past. Forgive yourself and others as a way to do this and you may find a huge weight lifted from your shoulders.

IMAGERY

A man lies defeated having been pierced by ten swords. This is symbolic of repetitive patterns of behaviour that have caused you significant harm or stagnancy. The fact that the man lies naked on the floor signifies how exposing and vulnerable it can feel to admit defeat and leave certain relationships/coping mechanisms in the past. You may not know who you are without this person or without this behaviour but your willingness to embrace this vulnerability will allow you to discover yourself on a much deeper level.

The dark sky is a symbol of the darker thoughts and emotions that this challenging period of time may bring up for you. Allow these emotions to rise up and to flow through you. Pushing them away or avoiding them will only cause you to repeat the cycle.

The sun is setting/rising in the background, a reminder that with every ending comes a new beginning. This symbolizes being at the dawn of something new.

Page of Swords

KEY WORDS
Insight
Curiosity
Eagerness
Intellectual innovation
Important or unexpected news

CARD MEANING

The Page of Swords often represents somebody who is almost too smart for their own good – the kind of person who wants to know everything, and wants to know it now. The card hints at the ability to learn new information and absorb it quickly, especially when it is something that you are interested in.

When the Page of Swords appears in a reading, it is asking you to have an openness to learning. You may already have a wealth of knowledge on a topic that you have been sitting on, unused, and now could be the perfect time for you to put that into practice while also learning more. This card can also highlight your ability to share your knowledge with others in a way that is both logical and fresh/innovative. This card has a 'prodigy' energy about it and can therefore represent visionary qualities.

This card sometimes represents the unexpected, but signifies that you are more than capable of navigating this because of your 'seeking' and 'learning' qualities. You understand the benefits of gathering facts, asking questions and seeking out mentors so that, when you find yourself face to face with a challenge, you have an intellectual grasp that will help lead you through it. You may lack experience, but your thirst for knowledge will help you seek out all you need to know.

So, what knowledge are you currently sitting on? Are you brave enough to ask more questions? Which mentors would be most beneficial for your development? Which topics grab your interest the most? These are the questions you need to ask yourself when this card makes an appearance.

IMAGERY

A young man grasps his sword, ready to meet any challenge head on. His body faces one direction while his head faces another. This is symbolic of the importance of environmental awareness and in being prepared.

Clouds are morphing quickly in the sky. This suggests that winds of change are blowing in!

The green and fertile ground suggests the page is able to bring positive change and forward movement to a project.

Knight of Swords

KEY WORDS
Bold solutions
Risk-taking
Innovation
Tenaciousness
Hastiness
Impulsivity

CARD MEANING

The Knight of Swords reminds us that, although having a genuine and passionate desire for something is great, sometimes this can manifest in the form of impulsivity, quick temperedness or carelessness.

Being witty and sharp, enjoying a debate or needing a mental challenge can be very invigorating experiences. This analytical agility can enable you to come up with bold solutions, creative answers or innovative remedies for any challenges that you are facing. However, sometimes this tenacious idealism can also be very risky, leading you to rush into things too quickly.

When this card appears, it is a reminder to have a balanced approach. Explore innovative solutions and learn from debates with the people around you but do not allow this to transform into any kind of extravagance or self-righteousness. When we feel very strongly about something, it is easy to be quick tempered or feel an intense emotional response. So, make sure that you are not compromising your integrity to prove any kind of point. As much as this is a card of warning, it also represents creative and risky success, suggesting that you have a lot to learn from trying new approaches or by learning from those who share different viewpoints.

If you have pulled multiple cards, be sure to take a look at the cards surrounding the knight as these can highlight whether this tenacity will work out in your favour or not. For example, if it is surrounded by cards that are very positive, such as the Ten of Coins or The Chariot, there will most likely be a beneficial outcome to having this approach. However, cards that hint towards risk or loss, such as The Tower or the Five of Swords, signify that you need to reign yourself in a bit.

IMAGERY

A man sits astride a galloping horse with his sword thrust up high in the sky. The image suggests facing challenges head on and having a direct approach!

The speed at which the horse and the winds behind the knight are moving signify a 'swift' energy and indicate that things are likely to progress quickly.

The horse is white, representing the pure intentions that motivate this person; you are being asked to keep these intentions in mind.

The wind is pushing trees and clouds towards the knight, showing that, despite opposing forces, he continues to charge forward with his vision!

Queen of Swords

KEY WORDS
Great wisdom
Power
Grace
Self-reliance
Harsh truth
Guarded strength

CARD MEANING

When the Queen of Swords appears in a reading, it suggests that you are more inclined to lead with your head than your heart, or that you would benefit from doing so.

This does not mean that you have to lack empathy or compassion. The Queen of Swords normally represents someone who has suffered their own fair share of sorrow in this life and has gained a lot of wisdom as a result. This card serves as a reminder that emotions can cloud judgment and that you would be wise to use facts as a way to discern what is really going on and therefore figure out the most practical solution moving forward.

This card can represent somebody else, so reflect on whether you need to be more open to guidance from a divine feminine in your life. The Queen of Swords is direct and straight to the point and can therefore come across as harsh or strict at times. The person guiding you may appear stubborn or rigid, but they have gained a lot of influence and stability as a result of this. You can trust them to be honest with you and give you a direct approach moving forward. If you are seeking answers, then they are the person who can help you find them, especially if you are feeling clouded with heavy emotion or confusion. Alternatively, you may need to be more honest with yourself. Do not be afraid to identify the ways in which you have been coming up with excuses not to do something. This card is a reminder that if you do not face things head on, you may lose respect for yourself or from the people around you.

IMAGERY

The woman pictured has a stern look on her face, symbolizing candid, if not harsh, honesty.

The cherub on her throne is a reminder that you can be direct and rational without it meaning that you are out of touch with your emotional side.

The butterfly on her throne is a symbol of transformation. You need to be open to direct approaches and new information.

The clouds and trees suggest that winds of change are blowing in.

King of Swords

KEY WORDS
Authority
Wisdom
Intelligence
Advice
Analytical creativity

CARD MEANING

The King of Swords represents someone who is able to control their mind and find clear answers to what is needed without any kind of bias or judgment. The card can represent a divine masculine in your life, such as a father figure, teacher, mentor or therapist. The person has authority and is well respected for what they do. Alternatively, this card can represent your own ability to be this mentor for others and hints at the value you have to share with the people around you.

The King of Swords is able to forecast events far into the future because of their vast experiences and the wisdom they have gained from these. The person the card represents has great perception, intelligence and integrity, and can be trusted to make important decisions or changes.

They might come across as cold or guarded, however their logical approach is incredibly successful, allowing them to have great influence over the people they connect with (for the better).

Ask yourself: Do I have something to gain from following a more logical and practical approach? Am I able to influence others for the better by offering upfront and direct approaches to their problems? Am I open to hearing advice that is fair, even if it does not bend in my favour?

This card represents the benefits that can be found from viewing a situation objectively rather than taking things personally. Make sure you are open to this person's guidance or are allowing yourself the opportunity to step into your full potential in this regard.

IMAGERY

The King of Swords sits facing forward, representing the ability to face things head on. He holds his sword in his right hand (the conscious and rational side) and points it upwards to the left (the emotional and intuitive side). This symbolizes balance and flexibility.

The upright sword represents decisiveness, yet the way the king holds it shows a willingness to be adaptable in his approaches.

The blue and purple of the king's clothes represent knowledge and compassion. A balanced approach is very important.

The throne is decorated with a butterfly, a symbol of transformation. Remember to be open to guidance or any new approaches.

An angel whispers in his ear. This serves as a reminder that, although logic and practicality are important, it is also vital to consider the spiritual ramifications of our decision-making.

The atmosphere in the background is calm, a sign that stability is near or has already been found.

Ace of Cups

KEY WORDS
Emotional connection
Love
Friendship
Compassion
Understanding
Giving

CARD MEANING

The Ace of Cups symbolizes the value of true expression and represents the valuable emotional connections that can develop from being true to yourself.

Whether relating to a stranger, friend, family member or romantic relationship, this card comes through as a reminder that connecting more deeply with others has many benefits. You never know what conversations or pathways might open up as a result of being more honest.

As this card represents an overflowing cup, it is a sign of being able to give more freely to those around you. You may find yourself in a phase of your life where you are either more energized and able to give freely or where you are feeling more inspired to do so.

This card can also be a reminder of the benefits of cultivating new friendships or love interests, so be sure to make the most of these moments before they pass you by. Remember, Aces are brief moments in time that need to be seized. If you receive an invitation from someone to go somewhere, then this card is a sign that you should go for it!

This card can also symbolize creativity, such as art, construction, writing or music. If you have had a new idea recently, or if one crops up soon, then you should pursue it.

IMAGERY

A hand appears from a cloud. The cloud is a symbol of the divine/spiritual realm and the hand represents invitations, offers and hands being extended toward you. The cup is overflowing with water, which represents your emotions. It is a reminder to share these freely with others.

The water flows into five rivulets, each representing one of the five senses and the importance of being around those who regulate your nervous system – that is, people who you can be your true self around.

Lotus blossoms decorate the water, signifying that you can triumph over your obstacles in the same way that a lotus blossoms from dark, murky waters.

Two of Cups

KEY WORDS
Connection
Harmony
Healing
Understanding
Intuition

CARD MEANING

The Two of Cups serves as a reminder of the importance of having deep and meaningful connections, especially one-to-one. There may already be somebody close to you who understands and values your experiences and opinions. This can be in the form of a friend, family member, lover or even a stranger. When you are more open with others, you can attract people towards you who are on a similar level to you and give them a safe space also to be more open.

This card represents the synergy we have with others – those in whom we immediately recognize ourselves, who we bounce ideas off, finish each other's sentences or just have a deep and mutual understanding of one another without many words needing to be spoken

If you are looking to find insight into a relationship or friendship, then this card is normally a great sign that you have mutual interests and can find a safe space with each other to grow and share in.

However, twos represent decisions and what you decide to do with this connection is completely up to you. If you want to develop this friendship/connection further then you will need to take action to ensure that happens.

IMAGERY

Two people stand facing each other, holding hands. The image represents the importance of closeness and emotional support. Each person holds their cup up towards the other, representing the importance of balance and meeting in the middle. This is a symbol of mutual commitment and effort.

A pair of giant wings hovers above the pair and is symbolic of the divine and how this connection has the ability to progress them both spiritually.

Winding snakes lead up to the wings, signifying growth, progress and the initiation of something important.

Three of Cups

KEY WORDS
Family and close friends
Support system
Spontaneous celebration
Healing
Rejuvenation
Unexpected joy

CARD MEANING

The Three of Cups appears in a reading to remind you that you do not need to deal with your struggles and worries alone. It can be very tempting to try and navigate your concerns by yourself sometimes, however this card reminds you that you do have close friends and family members who would love to lighten the load for you, if only you would let them.

This is a card of spontaneous celebration (or plans) and symbolizes the importance of letting your hair down every once in a while to revel in the love and joy of the people around you. You may have been taking yourself too seriously and need to let yourself unwind and share laughter with loved ones. When this card appears, you are being urged to find reasons to celebrate yourself or others. You are being asked to acknowledge the importance of your community and share the love and support of those around you.

There is purpose in our being social animals and even if you are more introverted, do not forget that we can lift each other up and support each other in times of need. Animals are born with the innate ability to do what they need to survive. Giraffes can walk. Snakes can bite. Humans can cry . . . for help! You do not have to do everything alone. You are not supposed to.

This card can also be a sign of unexpected joy, such as the announcement of a promotion, engagement, pregnancy or other major life milestone.

IMAGERY

Three people raise their cups up in celebration. This is a reminder for you to find a reason to share success and joy with others.

The three figures dance around with merriment, reminding you not to take yourself or others too seriously. Find the time to let your hair down and be silly.

The food surrounding the trio represents a feast. Perhaps think about hosting a last-minute dinner party.

The clear sky symbolizes the clarity you can find after spending time with loved ones.

Four of Cups

KEY WORDS
Boredom
Discontentment
Listlessness
Stagnation
Disillusionment

CARD MEANING

The Four of Cups asks you to reflect on the ways in which you are failing to appreciate what is right in front of you and are fixating on the past. It could relate to a relationship that has changed, an event in which you felt emotionally stranded, or simply that you are focusing on what you should have done instead of what you can do. Although self-reflection can be great, mulling things over too much can lead to melancholy.

This card symbolizes the discontentment that can arise when the initial excitement and anticipation of something wears off. Something may not be as it first appeared, and you may find yourself needing to face the reality of a situation.

This card also represents the thin line between self-reflection and disillusionment and is a reminder to shake off any self-pity that may be accumulating. Instead, it is time to review the options available to you. They might not be tempting, but do not lose sight of their value just because you wish for something else. Someone may extend a hand to you, and you may not feel inclined to accept, however do not be too quick to brush away other people's efforts. Sometimes these are divinely timed, and it could be a mistake to dismiss them.

Gratitude practices are known for helping people break out of stagnancy. If you focus on lack, all you will see is lack. If you focus on abundance, all you will find is abundance. This card highlights the importance of having the right mindset. It is time to reflect on your own.

IMAGERY

A young man sits by a tree lost in thought. This represents how easy it can be to become self-absorbed and not necessarily aware of the reality of the options that are available to you.

The man gazes at three empty cups – a sign that you are channelling your energy in the wrong places, looking at what you think you lack instead of focusing on what you have.

The man ignores the hand outreached to him in offering, signifying that you may be taking things for granted. It is a reminder not to brush aside invitations or offers of connection and advice. Do not be so busy looking at what you have lost that you do not recognize what is right in front of you.

Five of Cups

KEY WORDS
Significant loss
Grief
Despair
Flaws and imperfections
Endings

CARD MEANING

The Five of Cups serves as a reminder to deal with unprocessed emotions – whether this is about fully coming to terms with a relationship that has come to an end, or a physical bereavement of someone you love, or the dissolution of a path you envisioned for yourself.

When we go through major loss or disappointment in life, feelings of despair, worry and fear can arise. It can be very tempting to push these feelings away, however this card suggests that to do so simply allows them to crop up whenever they want. You may find yourself feeling less in control of your emotions or stuck on something or someone for much longer than needed. In order to move past this stagnancy, you must allow yourself to feel any losses fully. Failing to do so might leave you emotionally unstable.

This card is also a reminder to be gentle with yourself. The cups will fill again, and the storm will pass. The best way to get past stuck emotions is to work through them. Take this card as a sign that you need to charge headfirst into your feelings. Allow yourself to feel anger, to cry or to feel the reality of the losses you have had to face and may still be facing. Do not view these raw emotions as flaws. It is better to own your emotional state than to ignore it. Practising acceptance of your emotional state will lead you to empowerment, whereas avoiding it will allow your emotions to take control of you.

IMAGERY

A woman is slumped over in sorrow, signifying that you need to accept defeat on something and allow yourself to mourn.

Three of the five cups are turned over, spilling water over the pathway. Something of emotional value has been lost and there is no retrieving it.

Two cups stand upright behind the woman, signifying not all has been lost and that there is still hope if you allow yourself to consider the bigger picture (see what is right behind you).

A bridge crosses over the river in the distance. This is a sign that there is a way forward from these emotions once you decide to face things head on.

Six of Cups

KEY WORDS
Nostalgia
Pining for the familiar
Simple pleasures
Reminiscence
Idealization

SIX OF CUPS

CARD MEANING

The Six of Cups urges you to embrace the simple pleasures in life. It is symbolic of a connection to the past. Whether it relates to a person, object or place, you will find temporary relief by revisiting something from your past.

The card is a reminder to approach life with innocence and to enjoy feelings of nostalgia and comfort. However, you must remember they are temporary. This card can sometimes represent an idealization of the past and so it is important that you do not look at the past through rose-tinted glasses. As easy as it can be to remember the good times and want to go back there, there were also many challenges at the time that you may have lost sight of and it is important that you do not view this as a solution to your current problems.

Maybe it is time to go digging through old belongings or to reach out to an old friend you have not heard from in a while. Maybe you will find these people reaching out to you. You will find a lot of joy in reconnecting to the past but just remember to use these warm memories for temporary relief and then focus again on what is right in front of you.

IMAGERY

The six cups in this scene are bursting with life and represent the emotional abundance that can be found from a connection to the past. A young boy passes a flower to a younger girl, symbolizing the gifts that we can pass onto one another.

The adult walking away in the background serves as a reminder to let go of your 'adult' responsibilities for a short while and to reconnect to your own innocence and embrace a more playful energy.

The pair stand in front of a home, which is symbolic of stability and security. It can also represent a connection to a family home, a hometown or somewhere that you felt safe, welcome and free to explore.

Seven of Cups

KEY WORDS
Prolonging a decision
Procrastination
Distraction
Avoidance
Wishing instead of doing

CARD MEANING

When the Seven of Cups appears in a reading, it is asking you to reflect on the ways in which you might be 'wishing' instead of 'doing' or prolonging some kind of important decision.

This card is a reminder that, even though we may fantasize about having limitless options, this can sometimes make the decision process so much harder. As great as it can be to have multiple options available to you, this can also make the weight of the decision-making feel much heavier and tempt us to put it off as a way to avoid making a wrong decision. As appealing as it is to remain in a place where all options are available to you, if you procrastinate for too long, you will find yourself feeling very stagnant, drained and overwhelmed. In order to grow, you must commit to a decision and take action towards a goal.

It is worth keeping in mind that (minus a few complex scenarios) there is no wrong decision here. The worst thing you can do is remain in this daydream and waste your days not taking any actions towards your goals. Become clear with yourself about what you want to prioritize the most and take that first step. You will be all the better for it.

IMAGERY

A person gazes up towards seven cups, signifying the abundance of options or pathways that are available to you.

Each cup is filled with something completely different, suggesting that each decision or experience is unique, and one thing cannot offer what another does.

The cups rest on a cloud, serving as a reminder that all of the options remain in your headspace and are not grounded in reality yet. If you are truly honest with yourself, having these options may give you some mental relief, however you do not have any of them securely in your palm either (so technically you have none).

Eight of Cups

KEY WORDS
Soul-searching
Humility
Walking away
Fortitude
Embracing the unknown
Spiritual prioritization

CARD MEANING

The Eight of Cups suggests you need to look at friendships, relationships, environments and experiences that you have outgrown. It is a reminder that, if you want to grow, then you must put yourself in new, stimulating environments. Although you may have gained many lessons or memories from a specific place or connection, you must be willing to abandon some of what you know in order to create something more meaningful for yourself.

This card often appears when you do not know what your next steps are but have reached a point where you can accept that the current environment is no longer beneficial for you.

This card represents a willingness to venture forward intuitively, without knowing quite where the path is leading. You may know what you need to do but not be able to vocalize this very clearly. But that is okay, only you know what is best for you and you should trust your instincts. In order to get the spiritual satisfaction you crave, you have to be willing to let go of that which no longer serves you. This may come with disappointment and humility, but you know what needs to be done and now it is time.

IMAGERY

A man walks away from eight cups, signifying that a clear decision has been (or needs to be) made that requires you to walk away from something that has given you value in the past.

The path is not clear. This is a sign that you may not yet have all the information about what is coming next, but that you are not putting off your decision-making any longer.

The crescent moon serves as a reminder to listen to your intuition/instincts even if you do not have more tangible answers for others.

Rocky mountains stand directly in front of the man. He is not afraid to face these challenges head on. You can also see that these challenges are easily surmountable.

Nine of Cups

KEY WORDS
Contentment
Satisfaction
Fulfilment
Wellness
Success
Good karma

CARD MEANING

The Nine of Cups can have several meanings, depending on the context of the question or the placement of the card.

If the card appears in a question-focused reading, such as 'What do I need to focus on?', the card is a sign that you need to get crystal clear about what you want to accomplish and why. You may need to be more giving with your time, energy and accomplishments and focus on sharing the benefits of these with the people around you.

If the card relates to your accomplishments or strengths, it is a sign that you know exactly what you want, you have made progress in this area, and you are willing to share your success and abundance with those around you and should be proud of your efforts.

This is a card of generosity, sharing and connection. It represents achieving some kind of major success or reaching an important goal, and an understanding that this means so much more when you have quality connections to share this success with. This is also a card of thankfulness and gratitude and serves as a reminder to keep that good karma flowing. Remember to count your blessings and treat them as the gifts they are. The Nine of Cups only represents temporary contentment, however, so be sure to appreciate this moment of wellbeing while you can.

IMAGERY

A man sits beneath a display of nine cups, signifying a clear sign of success, accomplishment and emotional contentment. The man sits with his arms crossed and has a pleasant expression on his face. This shows that he is content with where he currently is.

The man sits on a wooden bench, which serves as a reminder that, although you might be comfortable, you will not stay comfortable here for long. Do not take this period of abundance and clarity for granted.

The man's white clothing is a sign of having good intentions and purity, both of which can lead to good karma

Ten of Cups

KEY WORDS
Commitment
Harmony
Well-earned blessings
Interconnectedness
Romantic fulfilment

CARD MEANING

The Ten of Cups serves as a reminder to honour the natural highs and lows that come with close, long-term relationships.

This card highlights the importance of empathy, compassion and emotional maturity when it comes to cultivating healthy connections with the people around you. It is also a reminder to build relationships that honour each individual so that everyone can gain something from the situation, and it can remain well balanced.

Living in harmony with the people around you can have such a significant impact on your mental, physical and emotional wellbeing, and this card highlights the importance of cultivating meaningful and mutually beneficial connections in your life.

This card is considered very favourable when it comes to romantic relationships or your family and/or home life. It often symbolizes someone that you can trust to stick with you through the hard times and who will also want to share in your accomplishments. It highlights the importance of interconnectedness and how we can all benefit from one another.

IMAGERY

Ten cups shine radiantly in a rainbow and are clearly a sign of divine timing, fulfilment and abundance! Two people hold onto each other with their hands raised up towards the rainbow in celebration. This is a sign of shared achievement and appreciation for one another.

Two children dance around with joy, suggesting an abundant home or family life and a symbol of purity or innocence.

Nature is abundant in this scene and a sign of a very fruitful and fertile environment.

The home in the background is symbolic of feelings of security and safety.

Page of Cups

KEY WORDS
Self-development
Self-discovery
Curiosity
Spiritual awakening
Wonderment
Sensitivity

CARD MEANING

The Page of Cups represents a developing curiosity that you have about yourself (or someone else) that makes you self-reflect on who you currently are and who you would like to become. You may even have had a new idea that you are curious about exploring.

There is an element of romanticism associated with this card. You may be trying to find deeper meaning in your life, relationships or purpose and have the opportunity to get more in touch with this side of yourself. This card is a sign to remain open-minded and to be willing to explore new pathways, especially those with more spiritual significance to you. As this card is in the Cups family, it is associated with creativity, expression or emotional/spiritual development.

You may find yourself being moved by things more profoundly and craving deeper interactions with the people around you. You are being encouraged to explore new ways to outwardly express yourself with these people.

This card can also represent unexpected surprises that inspire you into action. It is known as a messenger card and can come through when there is an unexpected love interest, pregnancy, engagement or other form of good news.

IMAGERY

A young woman gazes in awe and curiosity as a fish leaps from her cup. This represents the unexpected capturing your attention and sparking your curiosity.

The waves behind the woman represent the ups and downs of your emotional state and how these are always influencing things in the background. This is a reminder to be more in touch with your emotional state as this water imagery is also a sign to connect with your intuition, creativity and expression.

The blue of the woman's clothes is a colour known for calmness, knowledge and wisdom.

The youthfulness of the woman is a sign that she has much to learn about this area of her life.

Knight of Cups

KEY WORDS
Idealism
Love
Romance
Offering
Invitation
Declaration
Passion

CARD MEANING

When the Knight of Cups appears in a reading, it is reminding you that having a connection to your romantic or emotional side is not the worst thing in the world. This card quite literally represents wearing your heart on your sleeve and suggests you should put yourself out there. Whether in regard to a romantic relationship or your career, people will be able to recognize your compassion and vulnerability and will ultimately appreciate your candour and openness.

As much as this card represents passion, romanticism and love, there are several idealistic qualities associated with this card that you need to reflect on. Leading with your heart is never a bad quality to have, but it is important that you try to let go of the need to impress others. When going into a job interview or first date, resist the feeling that you need to appear on top of everything. Your willingness to ask questions and learn more about the role or person will give you more information about them and prevent you from rushing into anything without thinking about it first.

This card shows that you are finally willing to spring into action with an idea and take steps towards what you want. Do not be afraid to explore new opportunities and connections. The card can also symbolize another person coming forward with an offer of love, companionship or a work opportunity. It is a sign of pure intentions and therefore you can most likely trust them.

IMAGERY

A man holds a cup up in front of his heart, symbolic of a message from the heart. His horse is moving forward gracefully, a sign of dignity and poise.

The white colour of the horse is symbolic of purity, innocence and spiritual connection.

A slow-winding river leads into the distance, representing a connection to your emotions, intuition and expression.

The rest of the land appears barren and is a sign that this new idea or approach can create life and meaning in the most unlikely of places.

Queen of Cups

KEY WORDS
Nurturing
Compassion
Wisdom
Mother figure
Empathy
Devotion

CARD MEANING

In a reading, the Queen of Cups is urging you to connect more with your feminine energy. Whether this is within yourself or with somebody close to you, the compassion and understanding that you will gain from this divine feminine connection will be important for your current journey.

This card can represent somebody close to you, who understands you better than you know yourself. This person is normally a mother, sister, close female companion or potential love connection that has your best interests at heart. It is somebody who is very in touch with their emotions and is able to anticipate your needs – maybe even better than you are. They have experienced their own fair share of adversity in love and life, and probably have a lot of valuable wisdom to give to the relationship or your current struggles. Be willing to reach out and ask for advice from this person.

The card represents somebody who believes in you, who understands what you are capable of and who wants you to explore your full potential. They are not interested in holding you back, wasting your time or judging you harshly. This card can sometimes represent qualities within yourself that need your attention and you may need to show yourself a bit more compassion. You may be underestimating yourself, your abilities or worthiness.

This card can also represent your own ability to offer the same kind of support to the people around you. It is a sign of empathy, intuition and a natural ability to understand others. You may be a nurturing figure to those around you and this card can serve as a reminder to recognize that gift.

This card is a reminder that love does not come without pain and that success does not come without failure. Be willing to accept your losses and move forward with the trust that things will find a way of working themselves out.

If you neglect your connection to these feminine aspects then you may find yourself trying to control every outcome, getting more stressed out in general and potentially losing touch with your emotions or closing yourself off to others. With the appearance of this card, reach out to a female in your life and be willing to explore this deeper side of yourself.

IMAGERY

A powerful woman sits on her throne and represents somebody who is more than qualified to give advice in regard to your romantic or emotional life. She may also represent your own gifts in this area.

The queen gazes at her jewelled cup – a sign of wisdom and success on her own emotional journey and representing all the lessons she has mastered.

Her white dress symbolizes purity and the colour blue reinforces wisdom and knowledge. These colours signify a calm, peaceful demeanour that can offer a safe place to explore and share emotions.

The queen's dress blends into the water below her and is a sign of her being very in touch with her emotional side and intuition. This person can offer genuine empathy and is an example of the powerful side of being in touch with your emotions.

King of Cups

KEY WORDS
Protection
Loyalty
Empathy
Dignity
Conviction
Father figure

CARD MEANING

When the King of Cups appears in a reading, it is normally a sign that you have gained a considerable amount of emotional maturity and have no desire to allow your emotions to run the show. The card represents the need to accept anything outside of your control as a way to find a more peaceful and compassionate approach with others.

The card is asking you not to be so reactive and to use your compassion and intuition to help you carry yourself in a well-balanced and dignified way. Your emotion and logic may be out of step, and the card is urging you to consider where you are in this equation.

Representing someone who is able to sit calm through a raging storm, the King of Cups can also appear as a mentor or guide for you. It stands for a person who is warm, kind and generous with their time and attention, specifically when it comes to the people they care about. They value empathy, compassion and understanding and this is the kind of person who makes the people around them feel seen, heard and appreciated by others.

Relationships are of the utmost importance here, which is why this card is known as the 'divine father'. It is symbolic of a person being protective, loyal and fair and not afraid to support the people they care about. They can often show up for you during a time of need and bring other people to your cause. You may need to prioritize your connection to others at this time.

This card can also represent a connection to creative expression such as art, music and culture.

IMAGERY

A man sits confidently on his throne and is a sign of authority and self-mastery. He sits at ease, despite the tumultuous water around him. This is a reminder for you not to let your environment govern your emotional state.

The king does not even look at his cup. This is a sign that he has mastered his emotions already and need not focus so much on this aspect; he has more attention for the people around him.

A fish leaps out of the water and yet he is not distracted by it, once again a symbol of self-mastery and the ability not to react to everything.

The king wears the colour blue, which stands for knowledge and wisdom.

The ship in the distance is a symbol of action and movement and can also suggest travel as this card represents an appreciation of different cultures.

Ace of Coins

KEY WORDS
Material abundance
Opportunity
Potential
Inspiration
Contentment
Grounding

CARD MEANING

When the Ace of Coins appears in a reading, it suggests you should reflect on any new ideas, opportunities or beginnings that are being presented to you in regard to your career, finances or personal life. You may have a new idea for generating an extra source of income, you may be thinking of selling or purchasing a home, or perhaps an offer of career development is about to be extended to you by somebody else.

Like all Aces, this card represents a brief moment in time that needs to be seized, so make sure you are open to any new opportunities or offers that arise for you in these areas.

Now is the perfect time to be trying new things with less pressure on yourself. Try not to think too far down the line and talk yourself out of trying new things just because of potential challenges that might arise. Although it is important to remain grounded, it is also key that you keep a positive and abundant mindset so that you can get into a state of flow that helps things to unfold naturally.

This card represents a lot of potential. There will be a reason why you have had this new idea (or someone has made an offer to you), therefore you should be willing to believe in yourself and your ability to create more abundance into your life. The time has come to stop playing small and start thinking bigger for yourself.

IMAGERY

A hand reaches out from a cloud and holds a huge coin in its palm. This is a sign that you are being offered a new opportunity to improve your finances or home life in general. Are you going to grab this opportunity before it passes you by? It is right here in front of you and all you have to do is decide that you want to grab it. It is simply waiting for you to take action.

The landscape is lush and a pathway leads up to an archway, signalling that this journey or decision has the potential to grow into something much more.

The archway is a sign of a new door opening for you. You just have to decide to go through it to find out what lies beyond.

The mountains in the distance suggest future challenges that might be in your awareness but that do not have any effect on your journey at this time. It is great to be aware of these, but try not to hyper fixate on them or talk yourself out of trying something new just because there may be speed bumps further down the line.

Two of Coins

KEY WORDS
Indecision
Procrastination
Juggling responsibilities
Determination
Inefficiency

CARD MEANING

The appearance of the Two of Coins in a reading suggests you need to reflect on the fact that you are trying to juggle too many things at once. Perhaps you have two different projects or career goals that take up a lot of your time and attention. Maybe you are juggling your relationships with your financial responsibilities and becoming spread too thin.

Although there is an infinity sign here, which represents your infinite potential, this card is a reminder that you need to be willing to prioritize your time more efficiently and that you could probably benefit from reducing your workload or responsibilities for the short term in order to be more productive and focused. You may feel tempted to try and keep this juggling up for a little while, however the longer you try to do everything at once, the more burned out you are going to become (and that is not going to be helpful for anyone involved).

It is worth keeping in mind that juggling so many things at once should only be temporary and is realistically unsustainable. In order to have stability, you sometimes have to release some of your goals or responsibilities for the short term. What do you need to let go of right now? What's taking up too much of your time and attention?

IMAGERY

A man juggles two coins – symbolic of trying to do too many things at once and a reminder of how unsustainable and precarious this can be. You could drop the ball at any moment if your focus is too scattered.

The water in the background is tumultuous and represents the ups and downs in life. It serves as a reminder that, sometimes, your emotions can impact or cloud your decision-making.

The ships trying to navigate these waters signify that, with the appropriate amount of focus and precision, you can overcome and conquer any challenges that arise.

Three of Coins

KEY WORDS
Collaboration
Teamwork
Resourcefulness
Skills
Craftsmanship

CARD MEANING

When the Three of Coins appears in a reading, it serves as a reminder that, sometimes, different aspects must fall into place in order to create something much bigger. Whether this relates to a team environment at work, a blended family or some kind of personal project, this card is asking you to remind yourself what each person brings to the table (including yourself) and how the bigger picture would not be the same without them (or you). This card can also represent different elements falling into place, such as funding, inspiration and implementation. It hints at the need to have a balanced approach and the success that can result from this.

So, when this card appears, try to be open to collaborative ventures and do not forget to acknowledge the value that you and the people around you all bring to the table. Do not be afraid to bounce ideas off each other and learn from one another.

This card also suggests that the best things in life take time and that commitment and hard work will always pay off. There is no need to rush or take any shortcuts. If you decide to do this then you may find the quality of your work/vision dropping significantly.

This card highlights a desire to make the best of each situation and how having this mindset can allow you to push past any obstacles or roadblocks. Focus on finding solutions from the people around you rather than trying to do everything yourself. Remember the Two of Coins represents trying to do too much at once and so this Three of Coins stands for your ability to be able to move forwards from that by allowing yourself to rely on others.

IMAGERY

Three men stand in a circle while working on a project together. The scene is a reminder that working with others is oftentimes very helpful when it comes to larger projects or goals. Sometimes you cannot do it without them! Of the three men, a young builder helps older architects to bring their vision to life. This symbolizes the need to appreciate what each person brings to the table.

The young builder represents the skills/trade and the architects represent the vision. This may even be representing some kind of skill, trade or vision that you can offer to others (or maybe need help with yourself).

Even though the architects are clearly more experienced than the builder, they still appear relaxed and confident in his abilities. This is a reminder that age or appearances are not always representative of the value that each person can bring to the table. Don't palm somebody (or yourself) off on appearances alone.

Four of Coins

KEY WORDS
Negligence
Resistance
Paranoia
Missed opportunities
Confusion
Defence

CARD MEANING

The Four of Coins is often a sign that you have prioritized your financial position and may have become hesitant to spend your money and are now missing out on many different positive experiences as a result. Perhaps something inspired you to start saving in the first place and now it stands frozen and forgotten. Or maybe you have lost touch with the joy and inspiration that motivated you to start saving in the first place.

As the number four and coins both represent stability, there is no doubt that your finances are secure. So, what's stopping you? Fear? Paranoia? This card often represents a lack of connection to what really matters and that you are prioritizing money over everything else. Having too tight a grip on your finances can lead you to feelings of stagnancy and cause unnecessary resistance for you. You may need to loosen up your grip a little and prioritize spending your money on things that bring you joy and connection. Remember that money comes and goes but some opportunities are only fleeting. It is time to pay attention to your relationship with money and how this is negatively impacting your experience.

IMAGERY

A man balances a coin on his head. He very clearly has money on the forefront of his mind. He clutches onto his coins in a very protective manner, showing us that he is trying his best to hold on to what he has but has ultimately become paralyzed and stuck as a result. He is so attached to his money that he cannot really move or do anything without the fear of losing it.

The city pictured in the background suggests that the man has become separated from other people and is isolated as a result. Is your attitude towards money starting to affect your personal relationships?

Five of Coins

KEY WORDS
Hardship
Embarrassment
Shame
Isolation
Poverty
Pride
Negative mindset

CARD MEANING

When the Five of Coins appears in a reading, it is asking you to reflect on ways in which you might be letting your own ego get in the way of asking others for help. When faced with a hardship of some kind, you might be tempted to avoid taking full ownership of your struggles and the severity of them. This card is a sign that you could really benefit from putting your shame and embarrassment to one side and reaching out to others for support.

This card symbolizes the most humbling challenges we go through in life, such as losing a job, financial security or experiencing any kind of fall from grace (it can also represent having a fear of any of the above). It stands for the events in life that cause a massive blow to self-esteem.

A fear of rejection may also contribute to this, or you may have a limiting belief system that is telling you 'Nobody cares' or 'Things will never change' and so it is important that you reflect on the story that you are telling yourself about money, and how you feel about leaning on others for support. You can rewrite this story at any point and take back your own power by refusing to let your pride run the show.

It is important to remember that we all go through hardship in life, whether it is financial, relational or related to health. Therefore, this card is an important reminder that there is nothing to be embarrassed about when going through any of these. It can truly happen to anyone at any time and sometimes it is beyond even our own control. It can be very easy to let your pride get in the way of asking for help, especially when you find yourself in a place that you feel ashamed of, but this card is a reminder that help is nearby, if only you would reach out for it.

Try to focus on the support that you do have available and the things that you can be grateful for, as your mindset can impact your reality significantly. Are you isolating yourself from others because you feel ashamed? Do you not trust that other people will help you? Or that they want to help you? What story are you currently telling yourself about your struggles or fears? It is time to rewrite this.

IMAGERY

Two people walk outside in the cold, exposed to the elements. The scene represents a period of vulnerability in a harsh and unforgiving environment.

The person on the left is injured and symbolizes your ego being bruised.

The person on the right is wrapped in a blanket, signifying that you may not want the world to see you and are trying to find comfort in anonymity.

Behind the pair stands a church, its window a sign that help and compassion are nearby if only you would ask for it.

Six of Coins

KEY WORDS
Balance
Giving and receiving
Gifts
Generosity
Gratitude

CARD MEANING

The Six of Coins is an important reminder that there are times in life where we are all in need of assistance. Sometimes you will be the giver, and sometimes you will be the receiver. So, this card asks you two questions: Are you able to give to others freely without judgment? Are you able to receive from others without embarrassment or shame?

Since this card follows the Five of Coins, you may be willing, finally, to put your shame and embarrassment aside, to reach out for help and accept it. Or, you may have been helped by someone else in the past and now it is your turn to share the gift of giving.

Whether it is your time, money, energy or effort, giving freely to others can be very rewarding and is a great way to accumulate good karma (although you should not do it just for this reason, of course).

This card serves as a reminder to accept gifts with graciousness and gratitude, but to view this as temporary and to be prepared to put in the hard work to get yourself back on your feet. There is nothing to be ashamed of about needing help, however you must use these gifts to become more self-sustainable moving forwards. This is also a reminder not to overextend yourself to others too. Do not allow anyone to become too dependent on you as this is not helpful either.

IMAGERY

A woman generously offers money to someone who is clearly in need of assistance. This is a reminder to be charitable and non-judgmental of those in need. You may even be on the other end of this equation, and need to be willing to accept help from those who can afford to give it.

The woman holds balancing scales in her other hand – a reminder that giving and receiving is a balancing act. You must not overextend yourself, but you should not hold yourself back from giving either. You also should not hold back from asking for help, but you should not consistently rely on others.

Six coins shine radiantly above the scene. This is a reminder that wealth and help are always available, you just have to know where to look for them.

Seven of Coins

KEY WORDS
Dedication
Cultivation
Commitment
Nurturing
Patience
Security

CARD MEANING

The Seven of Coins represents your ability to show up for yourself in a dedicated manner, especially when it comes to your career. This card shows that you are not afraid to roll your sleeves up, do the dirty work and see a job through to the end. You understand that hard work and labour now will lead to rewards later.

This card hints at cultivation and a period of time in which you may have been assessing and reflecting on how much time, effort, hard work and money you have put into a project, relationship or business venture. You may be eager to take things to the next level or to take a risk, however, like a farmer tending to their crop, it is important to remember that the best things in life take time and that if you try to rush the process for a 'quick win', you may end up compromising all of your hard work and lose everything.

When this card appears, it is not the time to be taking risks or making gambles. Slow and steady commitment will lead to much greater rewards.

This card is a reminder to trust the process and keep pushing forwards. You have taken something from a mere idea to creating something of immense value and you should be proud of your hard work and dedication. Keep committed and stick to your plan.

IMAGERY

A man takes a break from working in the hot sun to gaze at his crop. This is a reminder to stop and reflect on how far you have already come. Something was once just a seed and now it is a reality! Remember to take a breather so that you can recharge and do not forget to appreciate all the progress you have already made.

The man looks tired, almost as if he is over it. This represents the exhaustion and fatigue you might be facing in your own endeavours and the temptation to give up and go for an easier win. The initial excitement or thrill may have worn off, however you are close to creating something very sustainable and rewarding for yourself if you can keep pushing forwards.

The clear sky is a sign that everything is on track, and that there is a clear path for you moving forwards.

The small mountains in the very far distance symbolize future challenges. However, you can rest and relax where you are now and trust that you have what it takes to push through this slump and persevere.

Eight of Coins

KEY WORDS
Skilled labour or craft
Learning
Repetition
Focus
Mastery
Skill development

CARD MEANING

The Eight of Coins asks you to consider developing your skill set. Whether this is for your career development or just for fun, you probably already have a knack (or passion) for something and this card urges you to explore it further. Be open to any new learning opportunities that come your way (or seek them out) and commit yourself to noticing the smaller details that might otherwise be overlooked by others.

It may become repetitive in nature and may even be a bit boring at times, however try to remind yourself of the rewards you will reap from this refined skill set. Not only will you become more efficient and skilled at what you do, but you will also be able to add your own unique touch on things and have a sense of pride and accomplishment in your work. Extreme focus and discipline will allow you to refine your craft and will set you apart from the rest.

This card is a sign that you need to slow down, focus on the details and enjoy the work for the love of it. As much as this card represents career development, it also suggests you should learn about the things you enjoy, for the fun of it.

If you are already talented in a specific area, this card is a sign that you should think about taking things to the next level. If you are unsure about your current skill set, this could be representing some untapped potential that you are sitting on.

IMAGERY

A man focuses intently on his project, symbolic of being in the flow and not allowing yourself to get distracted. The fact that he has made the same thing over and over again shows the rewards of repetition, discipline and productivity.

His hands working with tools represent an element of craftsmanship and can symbolize being skilled with your hands.

The houses in the distance serve as a reminder to stay focused and not allow other people to distract you away from your goals. You may also need to venture outside of your comfort zone a little bit.

Nine of Coins

KEY WORDS
Self-sufficiency
Independence
Individual accomplishment
Discipline
Success

NINE OF COINS

CARD MEANING

When the Nine of Coins appears in a reading, it is urging you to reflect on how much time, effort and dedication it has taken to get you to this level of success.

You may sometimes lose sight of your own accomplishments and progress, but this card signals that you have come a long way from where you once were. You should celebrate yourself for all the achievements you have gained along the way as it certainly was not an easy or pain-free process. Since this is a card of independence and individual accomplishment, you need to remember to express gratitude for your own efforts in this journey. Regardless of whether or not other people have helped you along the way, you would not have been able to get to this level of success had you not put in all the hard work yourself. You did this and it is time to recognize that.

This card is symbolic of the many challenges you have overcome to get here and of the steps you have taken towards building this future for yourself. You have put in enough time to be able to sit back and relax for a little while

IMAGERY

A radiant woman stands surrounded with lush green nature and nine shining coins. The scene signifies the abundance you have been able to create for yourself.

The beautiful home in the distance represents abundance and wealth.

The small snail in the bottom-left-hand corner serves as a reminder to reflect on how long it has taken you to get to this point and how much progress you have made. It also suggests that you should appreciate the little things in life.

A falcon sits on the woman's hand and is symbolic of spiritual and intellectual awareness and development.

The woman's red beret is a sign of increasing social status and a symbol of a rich life.

Her dress is emblazoned with Venus symbols, which represent the divine feminine and therefore signify that you are safe and secure here.

Ten of Coins

KEY WORDS
Prosperity
Stability
Devotion
Family
Legacy
Abundance

CARD MEANING

The Ten of Coins is a powerful card of completion and represents the importance of gratitude and reflection for all that you have accumulated.

A fantastic card for home, finances and family, this represents being in a position where you can provide for your loved ones or represents somebody close to you who is in this position.

This card symbolizes an accumulation of wealth that has come from hard work and perseverance. It can sometimes even hint at a legacy that is left for you. Either way, it is a sign of having everything that you need and being in a comfortable and safe position as a result. It is a great sign for any kind of financial investments, purchases or developments.

This card can also represent the importance of family. You may have a tight-knit relationship with loved ones, or you may desire to create this kind of family network for yourself. This card appearing in a reading is a sign that this is possible for you and highlights the benefits of doing so.

When the Ten of Coins appears, ask yourself exactly where you would like to see yourself in ten years' times. The card has a very slow and gradual energy, so it is important to reflect on your goals and what you want to work towards and why. This might even highlight some areas of your life that have been neglected and with which you would like to reconnect.

IMAGERY

A man watches over his family and there are two white dogs by his side. The scene encapsulates the idea of breadwinner and provider and also represents those who are loyal to you.

The man's family members are at ease in his home – a reminder to be proud of your accomplishments and the ability to take care of the people you love (and vice versa).

The home is luxurious and stands as a sign of wealth, abundance and stability.

A coat of arms hanging on the wall serves as a reminder to honour your lineage, legacy and family.

Page of Coins

KEY WORDS
Practical
Preparation
Grounded
Enthusiasm
Inspiration
Curiosity
Training

CARD MEANING

The Page of Coins urges you to consider how you should implement the experiences and skills you have already gained into a new opportunity that allows you to evolve and grow even further. It represents putting your knowledge to good use and remaining open to learning more about something that interests you. You may have just finished college or another important phase of your career development and are now being challenged to leave your comfort zone and gain more real-life knowledge and experience. The page represents new beginnings or ideas that bring you inspiration and curiosity. If you are already well trained at something, the challenge now is to explore it even further or to follow new ideas and opportunities. This card is normally a sign that you are on the right track, especially if you are feeling the desire for change.

This card combines enthusiasm and practicality and creates the perfect conditions for something to flourish and grow. Embrace a 'student' energy and discover more about this field of work, or your own particular interests within it. Now is the time for exploration!

This card can also represent setting up your own business and is a reminder that, as long as you are both enthusiastic and practical, you have some good odds on your side.

IMAGERY

A young man stands in a field of blooming flowers. This represents new ideas that might be blooming within you and that have the potential to grow into something much more.

The man is youthful in appearance, representing a lack of experience in an area of importance and the desire, or need, to learn more about it.

He holds up a gold coin, peering at it with curiosity, suggesting that you might be starting to realize just how much wealth you can gain from this new venture.

The fields and trees represent an abundant harvest.

The mountains in the distance are a sign of future challenges that lie ahead.

Knight of Coins

KEY WORDS
Methodical
Organized
Dependable
Seriousness
Sustainability
Fussiness

CARD MEANING

The Knight of Coins suggests a need to reflect on how methodical you are being in your approach to your goals. The card represents organization, gathering facts, being prepared and having a strategy to follow. It is good to have great ideas but the actual implementation of a solid and structured plan is what will allow these ideas to become reality.

As boring as this planning phase may be to some, it can be invigorating to others. So, whichever end of the spectrum you fall on will determine the approach that will be most helpful to you. If you struggle with planning, you might benefit from reaching out to somebody for help. When representing somebody else, this card normally symbolizes a person who is trustworthy and reliable and has a serious but pleasant demeanour. They might even come across as fussy at times, however this meticulousness means that the long-term sustainability of the project is more likely to be successful. On the other hand, you may fear that you are being too fussy in your own planning, but this card encourages you to lean into this energy to help keep the unexpected at bay.

This card is the only knight card in the deck that does not show a knight in motion; it is asking you to stop and think for a second before moving forwards with something. It can represent big decisions and commitments, such as the purchase of a home, or movement and travel, and you are being encouraged to consider all of the possibilities before rushing into anything.

IMAGERY

This knight and his horse are standing at rest – a reminder that there is no rush and that you should be willing to stop and reflect on your next moves.

The knight holds up a coin in front of him, signalling that he is mulling over his finances or any decisions that need to be made in this area.

There are ploughed fields in the background, their repetitive lines representing a willingness to go over things again and again, even if it is monotonous or boring.

Queen of Coins

KEY WORDS
Dedication
Commitment
Generosity
Security
Resourcefulness
Self-confidence

CARD MEANING

The Queen of Coins encapsulates 'girl boss' energy but, regardless of gender, this card represents somebody who is hardworking, loyal, dedicated to their family and loved ones and who enjoys living a life of quality. Very nurturing and protective, this card often represents somebody who is a working parent, or who has the ability to become one.

This card suggests the need for a balance between your work and home life and is a reminder that you can have both. It is asking you to embrace your own way of doing things, even if this does not match up to societal stereotypes. Trust in your own ability to take care of yourself and your loved ones.

The card also serves as a reminder to be generous with your time and affection, and not to view money as a finite resource. It is much better to invest in meaningful experiences and to live a life of quality than it is to just save money or waste it on meaningless or mundane things. You may have a taste for luxury and there is no problem with this as long as it is sustainable. With this coin energy, you are being reminded to stay down to earth and grounded.

This card also represents leadership potential, or somebody close to you who can provide you with well-balanced nurturing, such as a mother, teacher, guidance counsellor or mentor. The card highlights the importance of being able to live independently with your own stable source of income, and to prioritize quality time with yourself. This way you will be able to show up even better in your close relationships.

IMAGERY

A woman lounges on her luxurious throne, a symbol of comfort, wealth and security.

The woman is surrounded with nature, a sign of fertility and abundance, and her connection to Mother Earth (remaining grounded).

She cradles her gold coin with care, signalling that she is able to nurture financial abundance and that this nurturing quality does not take away from her success, but adds to it.

Her long red dress is a symbol of power and potential.

King of Coins

KEY WORDS
Authority
Financial security
Material wealth
Tradition
Practicality
Caution

KING OF COINS

CARD MEANING

The King of Coins represents somebody who values tradition, hard work and practicality – qualities that have allowed this person to manifest material wealth, security and abundance. Even if they might come across as stubborn at times, they are very dependable and are a useful person to have on your side. This card may be representing qualities that you have, qualities that you need to embrace or somebody nearby who could be valuable for your own journey.

This person has a respect for the ups and downs of life and has gained a lot of wisdom, especially when it comes to business or financial matters. Their success has not come from innovative ventures, and they do not really care much for taking risks. Logic and common sense guide this person and therefore you are being asked to embrace this mindset.

This card represents great potential for business partners, ventures or anyone who you need to rely on in regard to financial or business matters. It can also represent a fatherly figure, or the potential for someone (or yourself) to be one.

The King of Coins has earned great riches and may like to flaunt this. As long as you remain grounded, there is no problem with this. Do not forget to be generous with the people around you and willing to help those in need. Stay on the path and do not worry about being innovative or taking risks. You've got this.

IMAGERY

A man sits on a throne decorated with bulls' heads, forging a connection to Taurus energy and demonstrating the man's authority.

He is surrounded with luxury items, which are symbolic of his wealth and material abundance.

He holds a coin in his hand, a sign of his control and influence with money.

The luxurious home in the distance is another symbol of his wealth and self-mastery.

His red clothing represents his power and authority.

A SELF-CARE SPREAD EXAMPLE

The following reading is an example of the advice for you if you pulled these cards and arranged them according to the self-care spread format on page 33.

1 Mental state
2 Physical state
3 Spiritual state
4 Current perception of self
5 Current direction
6 Heights you could reach

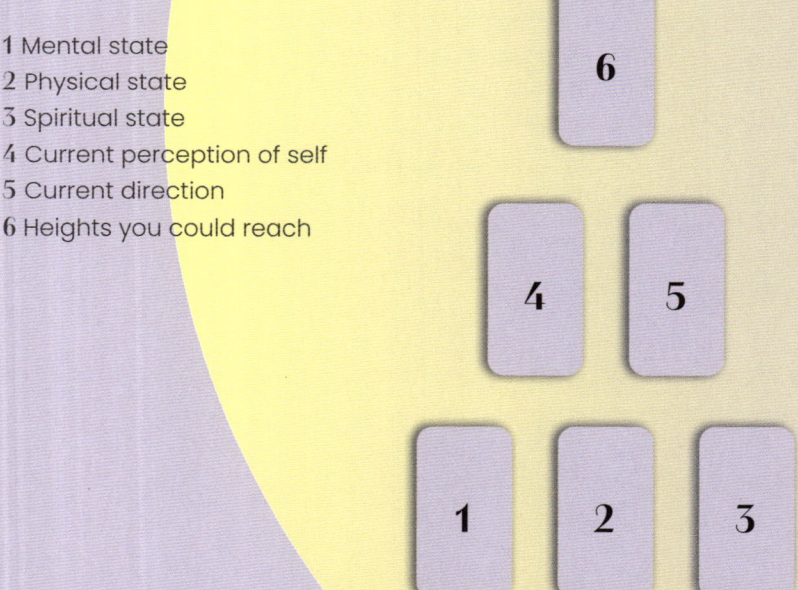

1 Mental state

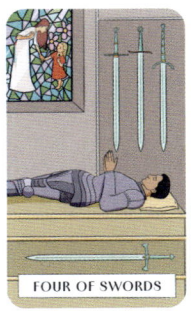

With the Four of Swords appearing in this position, your mental state has most likely been suffering. When the card appears in a reading, it is urging you to take some time out to rest and recuperate. It signifies a period of time where you may have a very busy mind, with your thoughts constantly flicking from one thing to another, with little to no rest. It is a reminder not to get too hung up on the past or fearful of the future, but to focus on what is right in front of you instead. To help your mental state, put one foot in front of the other rather than trying to juggle all of your concerns at once. Prioritize your mental health and do not take on any further commitments until you have had a brief pause. Although this card can signify mental struggle, it is not the end of your journey. After a momentary pause, you can pick back up from where you left off or maybe have a fresh start at something instead.

2 Physical state

As the Two of Coins represents a tendency to try and juggle too many things at once, perhaps taking care of your physical health has taken the back seat so that you can focus on your family or career. Or maybe you are on the other side of the spectrum and are prioritizing your health and fitness (or looks) over nurturing your close relationships. Only you will know which end of the spectrum you lie on, but either way, this card appearing in this position suggests a different approach is needed. Check in with yourself about how many commitments you currently have and whether these are sustainable. You may be juggling things successfully at the moment, but you have to ask yourself 'What is the cost?'. It can be tempting to continue doing things the way you currently know how, but this card urges you to consider a different approach. Ask yourself 'How can I bring things back into balance?'

3 Spiritual state

With The Star card appearing in this position, you may be experiencing a spiritual crisis or breakthrough. This card signifies a period of vulnerability during which you may feel exposed, but it also suggests there is an opportunity to get to know yourself, or what is important to you, on a much deeper level. This card encourages you to go inwards and reflect on your journey, inspiring questions such as 'What am I doing?' or 'Why has this happened?'. You would benefit from being able to identify and commit to what is most important to you and take small, practical steps towards this. Doing so will solidify your goals and purpose and give you a greater sense of direction moving forwards. Given the spiritual context of this spread, this card would signify a renewed faith system and a deeper sense of purpose as a result of a struggle (or period of vulnerability).

4 Current perception of self

In this context, the Strength card is associated with inner strength, courage and resilience. It suggests that you have the capacity to face challenges with courage and compassion, for yourself and for others. It highlights the ability to be compassionate but also firm, handling things with grace rather than power. True power comes from the ability to master your reactions and responses to your environment and so you could be learning to be more disciplined, patient or assertive. This card can also represent finally having the courage to show your true self. You may view yourself as authentic or having fiery qualities that are well managed.

5 Current direction

With The Wheel of Fortune appearing in this position, you may be unsure of where exactly you are heading currently or may have something in mind that is not going to pan out the way you envision at this time. You will probably face unexpected (or even expected) disturbances and delays that will shift your focus and attention towards something new. Whether this is a new job, a new living situation or a new relationship, the card is urging you to go with the flow instead of resisting it. Be open to change and see this as an opportunity for growth and learning. There are always positive opportunities ahead of you if you are just willing to seize the moment and be adaptable. This card is a reminder that some adjustments may be necessary for the bigger picture and to navigate these with grace. Having an open mind and the willingness to try something new will help with this.

6 Heights you could reach

The Chariot card represents self-control, determination and triumph over obstacles. It encourages a focused and disciplined approach that can lead you toward success and growth. It symbolizes purposefulness; having a clear sense of where you want to go and why and using your own willpower to get you there. This card is a sign that you could go a very long way with your goals if you decide to commit to them and stay true to your course. Life does not come without challenges, however this card highlights the fact that you are able to overcome difficulties if you decide to keep persevering in spite of them. The Chariot card is a great sign for personal empowerment, sometimes signifying running your own business, cultivating more independence or being more self-governed in general.

Now you have everything you need to read the cards for yourself. Wishing you the best of luck on your self-empowerment journey!

INDEX

A

Ace 22, 23, 24–5, 124–5, 152–3, 186–7, 216–18
Air signs 13
alchemy 95
Aquarius 13
Aries 12
aromatherapy 20

B

beginner spreads 30–3

C

Cancer 14
Capricorn 15
Celtic Cross spread 30–1
Chariot, The 68–71, 253
cleansing the space 20–1, 36–7
Coins 15, 17, 123
    Ace 216–18
    Eight 234–5
    Five 226–8
    Four 224–5
    King 246–7
    Knight 28, 242–3
    Nine 236–7
    Page 240–1
    Queen 244–5
    Seven 231–3
    Six 229–30
    Ten 238–9
    Three 221–3
    Two 25–6, 219–20, 250
Cups 14, 17, 123
    Ace 186–7
    Eight 200–1
    Five 194–5
    Four 192–3
    King 28, 213–15
    Knight 208–9
    Nine 202–3
    Page 206–7
    Queen 210–12
    Seven 198–9
    Six 196–7
    Ten 204–5
    Three 190–1
    Two 188–9

D

Death 90–2
Devil, The 97–100
direction of figures 27–9

E

Earth signs 15
Eight 23, 138–9, 168–70, 200–1, 234–5
Emperor, The 56–9
Empress, The 52–5
environment 20–1

F

Fire signs 12
Five 23, 132–3, 161–3, 194–5, 226–8
Fool, The 40–3
Four 23, 130–1, 158–60, 192–3, 224–5, 249

G

Gemini 13

H

Hanged Man, The 87–9
Hermit, The 76–8
Hierophant, The 60–3
High Priestess, The 48–51

I

incense 20, 37
interactions with others spread 34–5

J

Judgment 116–18
Justice 83–6

K

King 22, 23, 28, 150–1, 183–5, 213–15, 246–7
Knight 22, 23, 28, 29, 146–7, 178–80, 208–9, 242–3

L

Leo 12
Libra 13
Lovers, The 64–7

M

Magician, The 44–7
Major Arcana 10–11, 22, 38–121
mental state 249
Minor Arcana 10, 12–15, 22–3, 122–247
see also Coins; Cups; Swords; Wands
Moon, The 108–11
Mother Earth 52, 54

N

Nine 23, 26, 140–1, 171–2, 202–3, 236–7
numerology 22–3, 39

P

Page 22, 23, 144–5, 176–7, 206–7, 240–1
physical state 250
Pisces 14

Q

Queen 22, 23, 148–9, 181–2, 210–12, 244–5

R

reading spreads, tips 36–7
Rider Waite deck 18

S

Sagittarius 12
Scorpio 14
self-care spread 33, 248–53
self-empowerment spread 32
Seven 23, 29, 136–7, 166–7, 198–9, 231–3
Six 23, 134–5, 164–5, 196–7, 229–30
spiritual state 250–1
star signs 12–15
Star, The 104–7, 250–1
Strength 72–5, 251
Sun, The 112–15
Swords 13, 17, 123
Ace 152–3
Eight 168–70
Five 161–3
Four 158–60, 249
King 183–5
Knight 29, 178–80
Nine 171–2
Page 176–7
Queen 181–2
Seven 29, 166–7
Six 164–5
Ten 173–5
Three 156–7
Two 154–5

T

Taurus 15
Temperance 93–6
Ten 23, 142–3, 173–5, 204–5, 238–9
Three 23, 128–9, 156–7, 190–1, 221–3
time measurement 17
Tower, The 101–3
Two 23, 25–6, 126–7, 154–5, 188–9, 219–20, 250

V

Virgo 15
visualization 21, 37

W

Wands 12, 17, 123
Ace 24–5, 124–5
Eight 138–9
Five 132–3
Four 130–1
King 28, 150–1
Knight 146–7
Nine 26, 140–1
Page 144–5
Queen 148–9
Seven 136–7
Six 134–5
Ten 142–3
Three 128–9
Two 126–7
Water signs 14
Wheel of Fortune, The 79–82, 252
World The 119–21

ACKNOWLEDGEMENTS

Let me start off by thanking someone who may never read this, but who this book could never have existed without. Thank you Lilymae, for being such an incredible friend and for introducing me to the wonderful world of tarot. Without you, I wouldn't have grown into the person I am today and I'm so grateful to have shared such an important part of our journey together. Rest in peace and hopefully see you again in the next life.

Thank you to my Instagram and TikTok community. You inspire me to keep pushing forwards, to keep growing and learning, and have shown me just how capable we all are of meeting our greatness. I am so proud of you all and can't wait to see what the rest of this journey has in store for you.

Thank you to Emily for being my number one support at Quercus. I honestly couldn't have done this without you, and I am so grateful that you were able to see the potential in this book. Your support and expertise have been invaluable, and it is massively appreciated. Thank you for helping me bring this vision to life.

Thank you to Trisha, the amazing illustrator of these card designs. Designing a tarot deck is no easy feat, and I am so grateful for, and impressed by, your hard work and natural talent.

Thank you to everyone else at Quercus publishers who worked tirelessly to make this book a reality.

And finally, thank you to my Aunty Sharn for giving me a shoulder to lean on throughout the writing process. Having another author in the family has been a godsend and I appreciate all of the wisdom and insight you've provided during the process.